FROM CLAY TO CLASSROOMS

151 Howe Street, Victoria BC Canada V8V 4K5

For rights information and bulk orders, please contact
info@agiopublishing.com *or go to* www.agiopublishing.com

From Clay to Classrooms
ISBN 978-1-897435-67-0 (trade paperback)
Cataloguing information available from
Library and Archives Canada

Printed in Canada at IslandBlue's Printorium Bookworks.
Agio Publishing House is a socially responsible company,
measuring success on a triple-bottom-line basis.

10 9 8 7 6 5 4 3 2 1a

From CLAY to CLASSROOMS

An Architect's Dream to Advance Education in Africa

ALAN R. ROY

Agio
PUBLISHING HOUSE

For my lovely wife, Maureen

INTRODUCTION

A s a young boy in the early sixties, my awareness of the plight of Africa may have been limited to a paragraph or two in a social studies textbook, or a fleeting UNICEF television image of a gaunt Biafran child's plea for sponsorship. Growing up in the idyllic rural spaces west of Cornwall, Ontario, with seasons blending unnoticeably into each other, my brothers and I had no greater purpose in life than to look forward to the multitude of available local adventures. In the summer, we swam and fished in the warm waters of Lake St. Lawrence; in the winter, we skated on its thin frozen surface and tobogganed down the steep face of its dykes. In the woods on the other side of the creek that meandered through our back yard, we hunted rabbit, built play cabins and picnicked with friends at an abandoned rock quarry, our secret meeting place. We were oblivious to the daily struggles of millions of our counterparts in undeveloped countries.

In 1983, I was fortunate to experience a sampling of humanitarian work when an engineering colleague invited me to work with ex-president Jimmy Carter and his volunteers on a *Habitat For Humanity* project in New York City's Lower East Side, where I redesigned an existing 6-storey tenement building into sweat-equity-constructed apartments for disadvantaged families. That richly rewarding experience gave me the bug for humanitarian work, but it would be another 27 years before I had the opportunity to consider it more as a full-time endeavour.

The middle years of my life were immersed in pursuing the typical material entrapments of our western society but, at the same time, I noticed the work of humanitarian leaders achieving great strides in raising awareness and providing solutions to global disparity. Nelson Mandela stood firm and took South Africa from the extremes of apartheid through to democracy. I was particularly moved by the televised impassioned speeches of Canadian ambassador Stephen Lewis in his plea for help to turn the tide of HIV/AIDS in Africa. I admired the worldwide work of Rosalind and Jimmy Carter advancing democracy, human rights and economic opportunity, preventing diseases, improving mental health care, and teaching farmers to increase crop production. In the past few decades, hundreds of government and non-government organizations [NGOs], as well as private individuals, have rallied to the cause. Adlai E. Stevenson summed it up well:

"On this shrunken globe, men can no longer live as strangers."

Throughout the course of 35 years of architectural work, with 15 in my own private practice, I had often imagined a village school project in Africa as a refreshing complement to (or more likely, an escape from) the demanding western technologies of building design and construction. I pictured a simpler, hands-on, face-to-face relationship with a small community passionately intent on schooling their children as a way of improving the village's social and economic status.

In 2010, I felt it was time to shift gears and "give something back." I could apply my experience, and in the process, embark on an exciting adventure of discovery, not only of the mysteries of other cultures, but of self. The "kick-in-the-pants" moment came during a holiday with my wife, Maureen, in Mexico in May 2010, lazing by a pool, having just read Greg Mortenson's *Three Cups of Tea*, when I slammed the book down and announced to Maureen, "I'm going to climb Mount Kilimanjaro and build a school." I was a bit surprised at the conviction with which I spoke, but immediately felt a wash of contentment flow over me. My "gut" was applauding – definitely this was what I was meant to do next in life.

In September 2010, I made it to the top of "Kili", and three months later, I had built *two* schools: one in the impoverished district of Majengo, in the city of Arusha; and the other in the village of Gongali, near Karatu, on the road to Serengeti National Park.

So why choose primary schools? And why Africa? Although education is lacking at all levels in underdeveloped countries, it is at the primary level where children first develop the proper attitudes to learning. It is at this level that they can learn the basic social and practical skills needed to play a significant role in a country's economic development. And the choice of sub-Saharan Africa wasn't an arbitrary one; it was personal. I've always had an attraction to the visceral rhythm and beat of its music, the romantic allure of its landscapes that vary from the intensely humid jungles of the Congo to the dry grassy plains of the Serengeti, but I was also moved by the struggle of its people, caught between the digital age and the traditions of mysterious tribal cultures.

From an early age, I knew that education led to societal status and material security; all I had to do was get high grades, and the world was my oyster. But going to school was simply part of the daily routine, taken for granted, and when snowstorms covered roads with snow too deep for the school bus to operate, I was ecstatic. I didn't perceive education as a privilege. On the other hand, as a guest observer in Tanzanian classrooms, I noticed how differently children felt: they were extremely joyous, bubbling with enthusiasm, happy to be away from home, where they were often tasked at a premature age with household and farmyard chores. They knew that school was a special place that could dramatically change their life, and the lives of their families and community.

The lack of a healthy economy in Tanzania is exacerbated by the lack of the very thing that will promote it: education. Over 600,000 Tanzanian children do not attend primary school. The government simply does not have the funds for school infrastructure; it relies on private donors and non-government organizations. Suffering the most are many rural areas where the absence of water and electricity add to the substandard and struggling local economies. For the village mayors and district councils, a school project is considered one of their top priorities. Fortunately, over recent decades, hundreds of individuals and organizations like World Bank, Plan Canada, CIDA and UNICEF have been rallying to the cause to end poverty, provide health care and education, and stimulate the African economy, with projects ranging from new cross-country electrical power lines and substations to micro-financing loans to village women to strengthen local industry. It is hoped that education will be a strong factor in eventually achieving national self-sufficiency, with less reliance on outside aid. To realize this, hundreds of schools are needed, and the Tanzanian Ministry of Education is more than willing to work in partnership.

My undertaking of these two school projects, in retrospect, may have been somewhat impulsive, with the choice of projects seemingly arbitrary and perhaps irresponsibly devoid of government consultation, but the outcome was positive. We were fortunate that the local district education officers were pleased with the design and quality of construction of the schools, and were now eager to collaborate. At the Gongali school, for example, when it became apparent that it was too difficult and unreliable for teachers to commute to the school from the nearest town, Karatu, we agreed with their post-construction recommendation to build a teacher's residence adjacent to the school to house two teacher families. We provided the funds, utilized the same builder, and two months later, in February 2011, construction was completed. We were also fortunate that the schools were established with community directors and administrators to ensure continuing proper management and financial support. All too often one hears of schools built with good intentions, but years later are found empty.

Our work continues in Tanzania with more schools planned for construction in 2011. We have formed a non-profit organization, *Primary Schools For Africa*, complete with a board of directors, and at the time of this writing in May 2011, we had just received official charity status. We are now busy campaigning for donations to fund this year's projects. From the lessons we learned from the first two schools, we are properly researching new school projects, in full collaboration with the Tanzanian Ministry of Education, with local administration and management structured to ensure the successful operation of the school continuing in perpetuity, and with cost controls in place, so that donor funds are invested in well-constructed schools located where the need is most urgent.

This book tells the story of my amazing adventure – in the

hope that others will also be inspired, to become donors to *Primary Schools For Africa Society*, or form new fellow organizations building schools, since we have shown it to be a relatively simple and straightforward process. This book then, can serve as a practical guide; how to organize new school projects as well as how to build them using local construction materials and techniques.

The greatest reward for me has been the enjoyable relationships I have developed working with the people of Africa: the project managers, Jacob Slaa and Mathew Sulle, with whom I now have a close friendship, the staff at the Outpost Lodge base in Arusha, the taxi drivers, the interesting individuals I met who have potential school projects in their back pockets, the school teachers, the projects' local and district administrators, the builders and construction workers, and the villagers who celebrated with me and adopted me as a member of their community. A quote a colleague shared with me seems all too appropriate:

"Life everlasting is not in the hereafter;
it is the lasting memories in the hearts and souls
of the people we have met along the way."

Alan R. Roy, Victoria, BC, Canada
May 2011

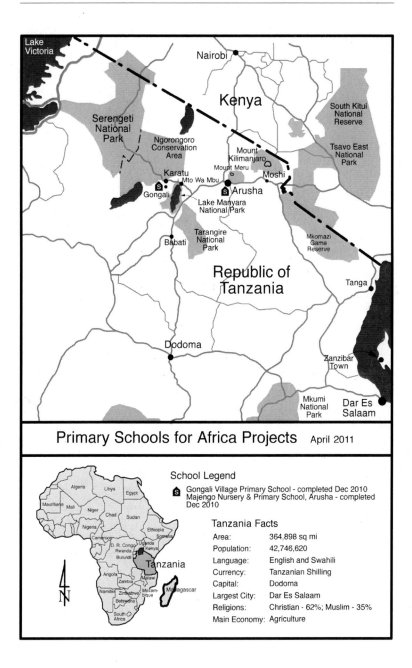

Primary Schools for Africa Projects   April 2011

School Legend

S Gongali Village Primary School - completed Dec 2010
Majengo Nursery & Primary School, Arusha - completed Dec 2010

Tanzania Facts

Area:	364,898 sq mi
Population:	42,746,620
Language:	English and Swahili
Currency:	Tanzanian Shilling
Capital:	Dodoma
Largest City:	Dar Es Salaam
Religions:	Christian - 62%; Muslim - 35%
Main Economy:	Agriculture

CHAPTER 1

KILIMANJARO

*"Mountaintops inspire leaders
but valleys mature them."*

– WINSTON CHURCHILL

Mount Kilimanjaro: "kilima" = mountain, "njaro" = sparkling.

On the sixth day of the climb, Suranga and I were on the final leg of the ascent of Mount Kilimanjaro, well into the much-anticipated, eight-hour grunt. A few hours earlier, at 11:00PM, our head guide Jacob Slaa had woken our four-person tourist group. We were 15,500 feet above sea level at the School Hut Base Camp site. Although Jacob had instructed us to get as much sleep as we could the afternoon and evening before, we didn't sleep well, perhaps because of the thin air and the cold, but more likely because of our anxiety level. We left at midnight, bleary-eyed, each with our own guide, to trek up the steep slopes of glacial scree and rock. The nighttime ascent was the most reliable way to achieve a clear view from the top during the 8:00AM and 10:00AM window: after that, the clouds always rolled in.

The previous five days had been, at least for me, "a walk in the park." The terrain had been well traveled by thousands of tourists before us. But there were always lingering doubts for all of us; a successful summit was not guaranteed. The main concern of the Kilimanjaro climb is altitude sickness which, if not handled properly, could be fatal. Jacob, however, had us follow the principle of "climb high, sleep low." We ascended about 3,500 feet each day, but climbed back down 1,000 feet to sleep – a process that apparently acclimatizes the body by pre-stressing it. Another concern was the dropping temperature as we gained altitude. We had started off at a balmy 77°F and were now at a frigid 14°F.

Our anticipation built day by day as we approached the final ascent. The first two days through dense forest and alpine meadow were comfortably paced. But our excitement peaked on the third morning when we awoke and witnessed for the first time the "snows of Kilimanjaro" that Hemingway had romanticized seventy-five years earlier. The flat-topped volcanic peak, streaked with its remaining slabs of glacier, loomed proudly in the distance. Each day, it grew closer, beckoning us forward, challenging us. We were above the tree line and marveled at the expansive panoramic views of the rock and gravel plains ahead of us, like an apron below and around the steep slopes of the peak. We could see lines of hikers miles ahead, like threads of small barely-moving specks. After two days of traversing the desert-like terrain, we arrived at the School Hut Base Camp site, eager but also anxious about the upcoming challenge.

There were 20 in our party: four tourists and a support team of local Tanzanians – 37-year old Jacob Slaa, his second-in-command Rama Kundi and a small army of 14 porters. We tourists carried only small day packs; the porters carried our gear, food, water and tents. Jacob was an amazing physical specimen with over 400 climbs in the last 10 years. A few years earlier, he had gone for the world record for the fastest ascent – just over 9 hours, held by a local Tanzanian, Simon Mtuy. Jacob's time of 10.5 hours, although nowhere near the record, still bordered on "superhuman" as far as I was concerned.

The porters were remarkably hardy. Their slender physiques belied an incredible toughness: they carried 45 pounds in their backpacks *and* thirty pounds of gear balanced (with no hands) on their heads. Despite minimal salaries, they were good-natured and enjoyed their daily routine setting up camp and preparing our hearty meals. While we worried about ankle sprains in our three-hundred-dollar hiking boots, they quickly traversed rough terrain wearing only sandals. And they traveled at twice our speed. They would break camp after we left each morning, and after loading up, catch up to us and pass us along the route, and then be at the next campsite with our tents set up and our meals ready, awaiting our arrival.

This was the first major physical adventure for my 25-year-old tent-mate, Suranga Suraweera. He was a New York scientist of Sri Lankan descent, who worked for a company that had developed a cure for prostate cancer by a process of blood sample radiation. I was enjoying our relationship, the 63-year-old mentor with the excited young novice who had never camped outdoors before. My jumping around and climbing atop large boulders along the way with child-like enthusiasm had earned from him my nickname of "Mountain Goat". I kept beckoning for him to join me in my antics, but he wouldn't. Eventually, he admitted he had a debilitating fear of heights. I couldn't believe it; here he was, on a mountain climb, with a fear of heights!

I couldn't sleep that afternoon at the School Hut site before the final ascent so, with nothing better to do, I decided to climb a precipitous rock outcrop overlooking the campsite, about a hundred feet up. I invited Suranga to join me, and he surprised me by tentatively agreeing. Twenty minutes later, at the top ledge, holding his outstretched arm firmly, I inched him forward to within a few feet from the edge. Although shaking with nervousness, he was excited and eager for success.

"OK, one more step. Don't look down," I firmly instructed.

We got within two feet of the edge and I said, "Now, look down."

His wide-eyed smile and exclamation of delight at his accomplishment said it all, "Hooooo-weeeee!"

Our grouping of eight for the final ascent included the four tourists: Suranga, an American couple (Debbie and Gary) and myself; as well as the guides, Jacob, Rama, Frank and Phillipo. The rest of the porters descended from the last campsite.

This last leg of the climb was every bit as daunting as the stories we had heard from other trekkers and from the tour company's website. We were on steep slopes of loose gravel scree and the next six hours were spent taking two steps forward and one step back. It was pitch black and eerily quiet. We were daisy-chained in line, our headlamps barely lighting our way, and hundreds of yards ahead the lights of several other parties zigzagged up the switch-backed trail. With the added weight of our winter clothing and backpacks, our thigh muscles were burning from the lactic acid buildup, forcing us to rest every fifteen or twenty minutes. I was also feeling a little lightheaded from the lack of oxygen. At the halfway point, the American couple was clearly suffering from the physical exertion and subzero temperatures and had decided to end it. There were only four of us now, Suranga and me, and our two Tanzanian guides, Rama and Frank. Jacob decided he and Phillipo would accompany Debbie and Gary to ensure their safe descent, but felt enough confidence in Rama and Frank to allow us to carry on without him.

We angled up the switchbacks as efficiently as we could, chopping into the gravel with the sides of our boots. My mind was becoming numb with the boredom of concentrating on one step at a time. But eventually it became comfortably zen-like, until about a couple of hours before daybreak, when Suranga interrupted my reverie.

"I don't know if I can make it," he said. "My legs feel like lead weights."

We tried to ignore the casualties along the way: "downed" climbers lying in stretchers with oxygen bottles strapped to their faces, their guide/porters kneeling alongside, waiting for them to recover enough to make their own descent. Several climbers passed us on their way down, each with their arms over the shoulders of a porter. And there were the desperate ones. We noticed off to the side of the trail, under cover of darkness, the shadowy figure of a middle-aged women behind her guide, her arms draped over his shoulders and her feet barely touching the ground as he dragged her up; she was determined to peak any way she could, unashamed.

"You're almost there, Suranga. Gilman's Point is only about a half hour away."

I remembered reading the psychological tactics used by guides in similar situations: break the task into small parts. If the climber can do five more minutes, he can do another five more minutes, etc.

"Just count the next hundred steps...."

Along with a little bit of tough talk, that seemed to work for Suranga.

At about 5:30AM, the sky was beginning to lighten, and a few moments later, when the sun crept over the angled mountainside, it brightened both of our spirits. We could see the first important milestone silhouetted against the sky about a half-mile ahead. Step after agonizing step, six hours after our start, we managed to reach it – Gilman's Point, 18,750 feet above sea level.

Gilman's Point is the common entry point to the rim of the dormant volcano. Most other routes to the top converge here. Dozens of trekkers crowded the top. Some were spent; this was the pinnacle of their efforts. Even though the summit at Uhuru Peak was only a short distance away, they were psychologically defeated and after resting, would descend.

The view from the rim to the centre of the volcano was spectacular. The crater drops steeply from the rim into a deep valley and rises to a large hill at the centre. Large chunks of glacier are scattered about several locations, the remnants of the massive ice covering of only a few decades earlier. The views outward from the rim are even more spectacular; we could see the gravel slopes falling steeply away below us, extending towards a panorama of verdurous forested landscape, its olive green eventually fading to a misty blue-grey at the horizon.

We traversed through remnants of snowfield and glacier around the rim for another two hours and earned another 590 feet of elevation gain. Then, at 8:40AM, September 9th, 2010, we reached Uhuru Peak. At 19,340 feet above sea level, this is the top of Africa. After seven days of trekking through virtually every ecosystem on Earth – tropical jungle, savannah, alpine moorland, deserts, rock, scree, snowfield and finally glacier – we had made it. From the summit, we were treated to an amazing panorama of 10-storey high "chunks" of glacier still managing to cling to the peak; massive crumbling walls of ice which, by some predictions, will no longer exist in as few as 10 years. The "njaro" (sparkling) in Kilimanjaro would be lost. What would become of the name?

The spiritual and somewhat giddy elation we felt was soon surpassed by the reality that we still had to descend to the Kibo Huts Base Camp and then trek another seven miles to our sleeping site at Horombo Camp. Suranga was spent and had to stop often to rest. Not surprisingly, his energy level picked up going down the steep scree slopes. We were literally "skiing" through the gravel, 10 feet with every step. After an 18-hour day covering over 12 miles of climbing, we eventually made it to Kibo, and then Horombo, by 6:00PM, where Jacob and the American couple enthusiastically greeted and congratulated us. I'd never been so exhausted. It was truly one of the most difficult and yet most exciting days of my life.

After 12 continuous hours of climbing, the top of Mount Kilimanjaro.

Keeping with tradition, after a cold, almost-sleepless night at 12,000 foot elevation, we awoke to a quick breakfast and were treated to the ritual of the 16 porters singing the Kilimanjaro song, addressing each of us in turn. The final line to me – "Babu Mkubwa, hakuna matata" – translated as "Grandfather Senior, no worries." It brought tears....

I turned to Jacob afterwards and queried everyone's title from the porters. Suranga was "Mjomba" [uncle]. The American Gary was "Babu Mdogo" and his wife was "Mama". I was perplexed by the difference between Gary's title and mine, since we seemed to look the same age. Jacob explained that it was important for the porters to differentiate us, so they asked us how old we were, and since Gary was a few years younger, he was "Grandfather Junior".

During a casual conversation with Jacob and Suranga on Day 7, the final leg of the descent, I revealed my ambition and dream for building schools. I had always wanted to be involved in an African village project from the early days of my career as an architect. The tangibility and the simplicity attracted me: the immediate rewards of hands-on construction alongside an appreciative community would be a welcome break from the technologically complex world of my Canadian projects.

"This is a difficult life for my family," Jacob said. "I'm away for seven days at a time, with only a two-day break in between." He spoke English well enough to communicate clearly with us.

"What other work could you do?" I asked.

"Head guide is the best for income. For a few years I was a teacher. The classes were overcrowded because of the lack of schools. I was frustrated with the lack of government support and low pay, so I quit."

An idea was gelling in my mind. A little later, I asked Jacob, "How easy is it to build a school here?"

"Hakuna matata [no worries]. Many villages and even city districts do not have enough schools. There is no government funding program for new schools, but the government welcomes foreign NGOs and local private donors to assist us."

"There you go, Alan," Suranga intervened jokingly. "Come back and build a school. Call it Babu Alan's School of Motivation for Young Climbers."

"Good one, Suranga," I quipped back. "Maybe we should call it Mjomba Suranga's Academy of Mountain Fitness."

We all laughed.

I turned to Jacob and continued, "Seriously now, do you have contacts? Can you help me find a school project?"

I wasn't prepared for such a positive response: "I will help you find a project," Jacob said, "and I will help you build it."

"I will be serious too," Suranga offered. "Keep in touch, because if you come up with a project here, you can count on me for a donation to help fund it."

"Wow! Thanks, guys. This is amazing. But, Jacob, what about your guiding job?"

"I'll work out something."

We shook hands, but both soon became a little bit reflective, and we spent the rest of the descent lost in our own thoughts. After a 3-hour hike down to a waiting bus, we left the mountain, stopping at the town of Moshi for the tour operator's typical cheeseburger-and-beer lunch before being driven to our hotels in Arusha. The goodbye was very emotional for Suranga and me. We had bonded well during this trip, and had shared some wonderful conversations.

I woke up on Saturday morning, the day after returning from the mountain, to a phone call from Jacob.

"I have a school project."

"What? Where?"

"I'll tell you all about it… What are you doing for breakfast?"

After I hung up, I took less than a second to convince myself that this was indeed an opportunity for a new life's focus. *Carpe diem*. I was close to retiring from my thirty-five-year architectural career and welcomed the idea of a complete change of pace to do humanitarian work: it was time to give something back. My wife Maureen and I would have a lot to discuss when I returned home.

At the hotel's brunch, Jacob described in an animated conversation his idea for a project in his impoverished district of Majengo at the west outskirts of Arusha. He knew of a female school principal, Teddy Cosmas, who had a 4-classroom nursery school that was in need of expansion.

"Let's go and have a look," I said.

"I've already arranged for you to meet her on Sunday morning. But today, I would like to continue as your guide, and show you around Arusha."

With a population of close to one and a half million, Arusha is the third largest city in Tanzania. We spent the afternoon touring around, looking at markets and shops, with Jacob generally giving me a taste of the local culture. Although there is an obvious sadness in most vendors' daily struggle to sell produce and wares, a colourful, friendly and cheerful outlook balances it out. Lots of "Jambo, Jambo." [Hello, how are you?]

Jacob offered good information about his knowledge of the local building process; construction methods and materials, approval processes, local government structure, etc. We visited a local "building centre" located near the downtown Central Market area to price materials. What an incredible experience! North Americans would be amazed at the contrast with our big box stores back home (think Home Depot). Building materials – from sheet metal roofing to rebar to toilets – are crammed into a small shop the size of a tiny house, with excess products stored on the sidewalks and in the surrounding alleyways. The most amazing display was the large collection of roofing sheets, gutters and pipes assembled at the entrance, extending high above the roof, creating a sculptural work of art to rival that of any modern artist.

It was fun dealing with the shopkeepers to get prices on all the materials. By the time we left, we had a price for almost every building component, from rebar to toilet elbow pipes, a list that would definitely be very useful in establishing school project budgets as well as verifying builder quotations. It was an exhilarating, and exhausting, day.

❧

On Sunday, we visited Jacob's neighbourhood to meet Teddy Cosmas, the female principal of the local nursery school that catered to over 150 pupils. Majengo is an impoverished district of approximately fifty thousand people, crowded into Arusha's western outskirts: rough bumpy dirt roads, litter everywhere, home construction varying from mud/stick walls with thatched roof to concrete block walls with sheet metal roofing.

We met Teddy at her church entrance at the end of morning service. A "traditionally" built woman with a warm smile, she reminded me of a slightly older (perhaps mid-fifties) version of Mma Precious Ramotswe, the heroine from the Alexander McCall Smith novel, *The No. 1 Ladies' Detective Agency*.

She spoke no English, but Jacob translated her softly-spoken greeting words: "I was praying this morning for help for my long-time suffering pupils who have little resources to study, where the classes are overcrowded and mothers are single parents with no income. Are you the angel with wings who is descending to answer my prayers?"

I was overcome by emotion and had difficulty holding back tears. My smile in answer confirmed in my own mind, as well, that there was no question: This will be a project.

We went back to her school office and discussed her overall building program options; either a new school on an available local property for sale – for 50 million Tanzanian shillings (TSh) or Cdn$35,000 – or a second-storey expansion of her existing four-classroom school, or a new school on her own 4,500-square-foot property with classes for orphans and a craft room for destitute single parents to develop marketable skills. I offered to help with the latter option since the others were too expensive and

Teddy Cosmas, principal and teacher, at her desk.

complex and, considering the difficulties of managing the project from thousands of miles away, my goal was to keep the project simple.

After the meeting with Teddy, Jacob insisted I meet his family for lunch. Jacob's family is a little better off than most in the neighbourhood; his home, along with those of other renters, is part of a rectangular building with a centre courtyard adorned by flowering trees, flower beds and grassed areas, an oasis in the surrounding blandness of poverty. A wealthy landlord who occupied an attractively-designed corner building owned the complex. I met Jacob's wife Birgitta, their nanny, and his three children, Anna, Febu and

15

Muchu. They were very friendly and playful, laughing easily at my prodding and tickling. The kids were curious about me, and innocently stroked the fine hair on my arms, and played with the hair on my head, that stood in such contrast to their hairless arms and coarse curls. I was treated to a hearty, typical family meal: beef stew, potatoes, cucumber and tomatoes.

The next step was logical: visit Teddy and her husband's property to determine the project's feasibility. The couple own and live on a typical 65-foot x 65-foot lot in an L-shaped building that includes a space for several single parents and their children. At one corner of the property is a chicken coop housing a dozen or so chickens. In the remaining space, there are beds of sugar cane and maize. Fortunately, the L-building is situated at the corner of the property providing a construction space that made further building a possibility. Teddy, Jacob and Cosmas (Teddy's husband) watched with keen interest as I paced out the dimensions of the existing structures, sending chickens scurrying out of my way. I quickly concluded that a new 1-storey, 3-classroom building would fit. This greatly pleased Teddy, shocked at the speed of the events unraveling before her eyes. She kept repeating "*Karibu sana, karibu sana, karibu sana* [(you are) very welcome, very welcome, very welcome]."

When I was finished, she directed us inside her living room where she said a prayer of thanks and hope for our success. We hugged warmly and left.

On the way back to the hotel, Jacob beamed with excitement;

he agreed to manage the project, and would somehow juggle his mountain guiding with his new commitments. In a quiet moment of thought as we traversed the bustling city through traffic jams and close calls with adroit jaywalkers, a few doubts crept into mind. *Am I going to be able to pull this off?*

Back at the hotel, I reflected on my original goal; to build primary schools in villages. Teddy's project, a nursery school in a big city, although honorable, was a variation on the theme.

As I lay in bed that night, cocooned within the mosquito netting around the bed, my thoughts drifted to the interesting conversation I would have with Maureen when I returned. We have been so wrapped up in our individual careers that we had spent little time discussing "retirement" plans. Certainly, we could hope to look forward to grandparenting, gardening, more world travels, the idea of buying a cottage on the lake, book clubs, etc, but we often spoke of somehow giving back in a way that reflected our professional skills and experience. My sudden decision may be a shock to our present routine, but it could also lead to new adventures. I considered myself blessed to have Maureen as my wife, a woman with whom I negotiated many challenges in our nine-year marriage. I felt confident that she would embrace my Africa idea.

❧

On Monday, I still had five days before flying home to Canada – enough time to call the local government education offices for information, if such places existed. I tried to contact the Ministry of Education to no avail. During my evening meal at the hotel, I queried the location from a waiter named Steve. His eyes lit up when I told him of my intentions to build a school, and he quickly suggested I should meet his brother Mathew, the hotel's restaurant manager.

After dinner, Steve took me his brother's office, an alcove in the restaurant, and introduced me to 35-year-old Mathew Gabriel Sulle. He had a short, compact build, and was intense, very bright, and articulate. Judging by the efficiency of his staff as he barked out orders while we talked, he was also very adept as a manager. His English was passable.

Mathew and I enjoyed a long conversation about the village of Gongali where he grew up, and how the majority of children there do not have access to education. A new primary school was badly needed for about 40 to 50 children. The prospect of education for his impoverished village more than thrilled him; he offered to volunteer his time to personally manage the project. I immediately liked him, and sensed that we could easily become good friends.

The pace of the events that were to follow was incredible. On Tuesday morning we were heading to Mathew's small village, a three-hour drive west of Arusha. While we were driving, Mathew was on his cell, phoning ahead to arrange a meeting with local officials to discuss ideas for a project. I thought, *I may have my long-held dream of a village project after all.*

The village of Gongali is in the district of Karatu Town, near Lake Manyara National Park, and it's on the main route to two large, popular safari regions: the Ngorongoro Crater and the Serengeti Plains. The trip was interesting, with us traveling through Maasai country, witnessing cattle-herding young men dressed in the famous colourful Maasai blankets, and later, near Lake Manyara, encountering a troop of baboons feasting on grass near the roadway.

"Stop the car," I shouted to the driver. "I want some photos."

I ran over to them.

"Don't get too close, you could be attacked," Mathew warned.

I quickly snapped a few shots and retreated. What excitement! *I'm in Africa – experiencing the wildlife!*

Arriving at the village around noon, we were greeted by Mathew's brother Pascal and his 68-year-old ailing mother who appeared quietly fragile and withdrawn. I asked about her health; Mathew confided that she was in desperate need of a serious operation but was awaiting the balance of required funds. Considering our previous discussion, during which time Mathew had been reluctant to receive any payment whatsoever for his potential involvement in the project, I thought the least I could do was offer him the operation payment, which was small in comparison to Canadian hospital costs, as a gift for his efforts. In return, he gave me a warm hug. He explained the event to his mother, and for a moment, I detected a glimmer of happiness in her sad face.

On the way to the meeting, we passed a group of villagers lined up at a watering station, a tap on a pipe sticking out of the ground. They would each wait a long time for their turn since the water was barely a trickle. Gongali and the two sister villages of Quuru and Bashay were lucky to have water at all, thanks to the brain-child of a resident named Claude Goi (as it turned out, he was Mathew's best man), who had organized the construction of a pipe distribution system from a mountain stream some distance away from the village.

The design was ingenious, considering Claude had no engin-eering background. But he did know that water flowed downhill, and that it was downhill all the way from the mountain stream to the village. Pipes that were installed in the stream carried water by gravity to a nearby large concrete tank from which it flowed though pipes to smaller tanks near the villages. From there, an ar-ray of pipes fanned out to various taps around the village. The low flow rates did not bother anyone. The close availability of water had been a godsend, considering that children had to fetch it be-fore. They had gotten up each morning at 3:00AM, then hiked (or run) 10 miles to the stream, returned balancing a 45-pound plastic container filled with water on their head, had breakfast, and *ar-rived at school by 7:30!*

The meeting was held at the Gongali Village mayor's office, a small plain unlit building no bigger than a one-car garage.

Seated around a small table were Peter Hayshi, the district vice-chairman for the three villages; Philemon Baran, the mayor of Gongali; and several of his administrative staff, all appearing a little on the serious side. Peter, a man of strong stature who exuded a quiet importance, was obviously the head honcho, and respon-sible for major decisions. After proper introductions, Mathew

The village water tap and waiting transportation at Gongali. The water comes via pipe from a mountain stream many miles away.

presented my intentions in Swahili while I anxiously sat alongside, curious about the shy fleeting glances I received. When Mathew was finished, Peter nodded his head. Philemon said a few words, and everyone got up to leave. They were smiling, except Peter, who, maintaining his solemn appearance, shook my hand and told me I was now a member of the village. With other apparent business to take care of, he quickly drove off down the dry dirt road, his truck swallowed by its dusty entrails. I guessed the meeting was a success. Mathew, smiling, explained Philemon's few words: "We will donate 10 acres of property for the school."

Philemon then took us for a drive to the donated property where a group of villagers were already assembled. Word about us had spread quickly. Adjacent to one of the main dirt roads leading from the village, the site was a large open flat field containing a shoulder-high pigeon pea crop that, amusingly, obscured all but the heads and shoulders of the villagers. This was to be, in effect, the village briefing. We gathered atop a pile of loose rubble and Mathew and Philemon presented the plans, this time with vigor and emphatic gesturing, while the two dozen or so men, women and children listened intently. Not being one to stand on ceremony, I still felt I should say a few words. I nudged Mathew and silently pleaded with raised eyebrow. Embarrassed at forgetting to formally introduce me, he gestured for me to begin.

"Mjambo, my name is Alan Roy, and I am pleased to meet you. I hope we can work together to build a new school for the village

Gongali mayor Philemon Baran, left; district vice-chairman Peter Hayshi, second from left; Mathew Sulle, right.

so that your children, through education, may bring hope and prosperity to your community."

The villagers solemnly listened, not understanding a word I said, their reaction a humorous mixture of confusion and respect.

Then, through Mathew's translations, we discussed the size of the school. Philemon's ideal was a minimum four-classroom building at forty-five students per classroom. Four classrooms were beyond my budget, but I suggested that we could start with two now and allow for future expansion to four, or six. We then discussed the location factors for the school; it should be as high as possible to avoid the low, swampy (during rainy season) area

Alan and Mathew briefing workers at the new Gongali school site.

adjacent the road, but not higher than the gravity-fed water supply system. I pointed out that a site plan showing the dimensions of the property lines would be very helpful, at which the mayor promptly ordered a villager to pace off the boundaries. He returned with "220 long steps x 240 long steps." (I wasn't about to question the legal accuracy.)

"Thank you. I can now produce a site plan for you," I said.

They also added a desire for spaces for gardens, sports fields and tree planting.

"OK!"

When the meeting ended, Philemon shouted at the villagers. They ran off.

"What was that all about?" I asked.

"Philemon ordered everyone to immediately start collecting stones for the building foundations."

I was both thrilled and amazed by their sudden enthusiasm. It was as if they didn't start immediately, the project might disappear.

Mathew, Philemon and I then had lunch at a local restaurant in nearby Karatu, followed by a visit to the local "building centre" to price materials. It was a repeat of the previous enlightening experience in Arusha; but as expected, the prices here were about 10% higher than in Arusha, so we contemplated ways of trucking in the material to save money.

The dusty ride back to Arusha seemed long and tedious, and again, in reflection, the doubts crept in, only doubly so now – two projects in 3 days. Yikes! What was I in for? Whatever happened now, it was definitely going to be an interesting ride. Many questions still remained, and I had so much to learn about the process of building in a foreign country.

The remaining few days in Arusha were spent obtaining a resident permit, setting up a bank account for the financial transactions with the builders, and writing instructions to Mathew and Jacob for administrating the tender and construction of the projects. Now I just had to go back to Canada, draw up the plans, get them to an architectural firm in Dar Es Salaam for review and translation into Swahili, if necessary, and forward them to Arusha. We were all set to go!

CHAPTER 2

THE CULTURAL GAP

"The man who goes out alone can start today;
but he who travels with another must wait till that other is ready."

– HENRY DAVID THOREAU

Typical building centre in Arusha with hardware hanging from the trees.

After a 30-hour journey by plane, bus and ferry, I arrived back in Victoria in the evening of September 18 to drizzling rain and windy weather, but the discomfort was easily overcome by the wonderfully sunny smile of my Maureen. She was as eager to hear about all the details of my adventures as I was to tell her. Due to the spotty Internet and telephone connections from Arusha, she was totally unaware of what had transpired in the last week.

The 30-minute drive home from the ferry terminal felt like 10 minutes.

"You won't believe what I've been up to," I said.

"Uh oh," she nervously laughed. "Do I really want to know?"

"Remember when I finished reading Greg Mortenson's *Three Cups of Tea* last spring and I announced I would start building schools in Africa? You didn't take me seriously. Well, guess what?" I asked.

"Hmmmm…" she mused, "judging from you being wide-eyed and hyperventilating…."

"Yup! I've lined up two school projects in Tanzania!" I blurted.

I paused for a moment, and then said, "Well, at least I think I did. I'll have to continue talks with my new friends there to see what's possible. The language barrier may be a big issue. I have no idea what costs are involved. And I'm not sure about dealings with their Ministry of Education; I've had little luck in the short time there to find contacts, let alone have discussions with them."

It felt good to be back, but before I could recuperate from the jet lag, I was treated to a wonderful surprise. Friends and family had been keeping track of my Kilimanjaro ascent through an Internet link set up by the tour company, and therefore Maureen thought that hosting a surprise party the following evening would be a good opportunity for them to congratulate me. I was thankful to have such a supportive community. The energy in the room was exciting and stimulating. We talked about the climb, the school projects, the wonderful Tanzanian people, their politics, the children... until my adrenaline petered out, and fatigue finally forced me to pack it in.

In my first week back from Tanzania, I managed to design both projects. It seemed like back to the drawing board as usual, except that my clients were not the usual sophisticated corporate executives or government middle managers with complex architectural programs. In contrast, I was designing structures no more complicated than a detached garage. But I had never felt more excited about a project.

The designs were finalized: for Majengo, a simple 840-square-foot rectangular building with two 24-children nursery classrooms and a crafts room; for Gongali, 1150-square-feet with two 45-student classrooms. Each building would have something that was not typical in most Tanzanian schools: indoor washrooms. This lack was probably due to the additional construction cost, and the scarcity of water in most regions.

The Majengo site had "city" water supply, but Gongali didn't. Drilling at the Gongali site was possible, but expensive, and successfully finding water was not guaranteed. I opted for the design

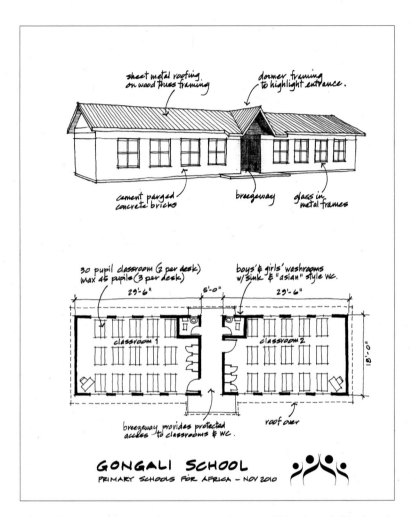

sheet metal roofing
on wood truss framing

dormer framing
to highlight entrance.

cement parged
concrete bricks

breezeway

glass in
metal frames

30 pupil classroom (2 per desk)
max 45 pupils (3 per desk)

boys' & girls' washrooms
w/sink & "asian" style WC.

29'-6"

5'-0"

29'-6"

classroom 1

classroom 2

18'-0"

breezeway provides protected
access to classrooms & WC.

roof over

GONGALI SCHOOL
PRIMARY SCHOOLS FOR AFRICA - NOV 2010

of an elevated water tank structure that could be hand filled with water transported from the village "tap" and, during the wet season, with roof water.

Waste water design for both projects would consist of a single- or two-stage septic system that was the best local standard:

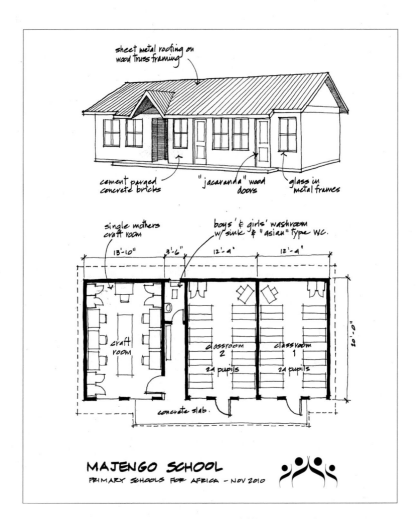

sheet metal roofing on wood truss framing

cement paved concrete bricks

"jacaranda" wood doors

glass in metal frames

single mothers craft room

boys' & girls' washroom w/ sink & "asian" type WC.

13'-10" 3'-6" 12'-4" 12'-4"

20'-0"

craft room

classroom 2
24 pupils

classroom 1
24 pupils

concrete slab.

MAJENGO SCHOOL
PRIMARY SCHOOLS FOR AFRICA – NOV 2010

underground concrete tanks that would be pumped out every ten years or so.

The technical detailing and specifications were based on what I had gathered from observing local buildings under construction in the Arusha region. The challenge was to marry the technologies of

Tanzania with that of Canada. Mud brick and thatched roof construction, traditionally used in the rural areas (due to economic necessity) was out of the question. These buildings deteriorated very quickly in the rains, often lasting not more than ten to fifteen years. I elected to use typical Tanzanian new construction for simple one-storey buildings consisting of concrete floors, concrete block walls and wood framed roofs clad with sheet metal. What I hoped with my designs, through good detailing and thorough specifications, was to build a structure that would last at least 50 years. That meant, for example, properly compacted foundations and footings and sufficient steel reinforcement in the concrete. I considered this an important aspect of the process of building schools, to ensure that the money from donors resulted in a solid investment. What remained to be seen, of course, was how the builders of the project would react to some of the plans. This would no doubt be a learning process for both sides. I was looking forward to it.

I sent plans to Jacob and Mathew and anxiously awaited their replies.

My communication with the school project managers was a little stilted. Mathew had been phoning every other day since my return to Canada; he was chomping at the bit to get the Gongali school started. But the conversations were constantly broken up by a poor phone connection, so I concluded that everything would have to be done using e-mail. The good news was that many Google sites translated languages, so I was able to enter English into the program and get Swahili. Then I would copy the translation into my e-mail. Perfect! He would get both English and Swahili. The bad news was the translations were often poor. I entered the Swahili translation back into the translation program to verify it, and I was surprised at the results. For example, I queried, "We need to design the removal of the toilet waste." The Swahili translation was, "We need the model to remove the filthy toilets."

I needed to get a good translator on board to ensure the nuances of our communications were totally understood. I called the Victoria Refugee and Immigration Centre (VIRC). They said they'd contact several available Swahili-speaking candidates and would get back to me. I also e-mailed the University of Arusha to establish an academic connection perhaps with an educator that spoke English well. I didn't know how useful it would be, but it could lead to other "connections".

I instructed Mathew and Jacob to get competitive pricing from local builders and to use their judgment to select trustworthy and experienced ones. My instructions for the bidding process were to have builders list all materials and labour costs. Within a week, I had received multiple quotes for both projects and was looking forward to the lowest bid. But two problems surfaced – the quotations were crudely hand-written, and they were in Swahili, making them impossible to review properly. I pleaded with Jacob and Mathew to appeal to the builders' patience and have them resend the quotations, only this time typed and in English. I was quite surprised when they complied.

The quotations' material list pricing was generally in line with the information I had previously collected. The Gongali school quote from a Mr. Fabian Amma was roughly on budget, but after an exhaustive review of Teddy's project, I discovered the lowest bid had missed too many items. That made us a little nervous, so we went with the number two bid of a Mr. Hemedi Iddi.

The cost for each project was approximately the same, around Cdn$15,000, with the cost per classroom between Cdn$5,000 and 7,000, a small fraction compared to our western construction, for the same education value it would provide.

The next step was to format some kind of contract that we would all sign to formalize the process. It should be in both English and Swahili, but what to do for a translator? I'd also been having trouble understanding Jacob and Mathew's e-mails. Because of their limited English vocabulary, the answers didn't always make sense. I awaited a call from VIRC.

My stepson Gavin, in the nursing program at Vancouver Island University, mentioned he had a female African classmate that spoke at least six Swahili dialects. Six dialects?! Which ones was I dealing with? As it turned out, she wasn't available, however, success was soon mine when VIRC called to say a possible candidate named James Wanjohi would be phoning.

When 48-year-old James and I met, we liked each other instantly. He had a wonderful smile, a deep resonant voice and an infectious sense of humour. I could sense his excitement and pride to have this opportunity to help his fellow Africans. He would turn out to be the ideal African consultant.

James grew up in a very poor family in Nairobi, Kenya, and from an early age had realized that only through education could he achieve a proper standard of living and be of help to his impoverished community. After graduating from the University of Nairobi, he lived for some years working in Tanzania as a middle management level government bureaucrat. His experience proved extremely useful for my school building efforts, and not only in matters of translation. In the future, he could help to establish the charity as an official NGO in Tanzania.

His first tasks were to interpret the "official" letters that I requested for my records from Teddy Cosmas and the mayor of Gongali, letters that officially stated their education needs, as well as the formal permission to build the schools on their properties. His second task was to translate the documents that would be used for administering the construction: contracts, progress claims and material receipts.

Sometimes things just fall in place. I couldn't believe my luck in finding him.

James has been in Canada since 1985. He invited me to meet his family; his wife Jennifer works as a mental-health nursing aide; his three children are doing well, one is in university and the other two are in high school.

We soon became very good friends. One evening we attended a slide show presented by a Victoria couple, Bill German and his wife

Joan, whose charity provides financial support for young Kenyan teens to attend high school. Slides of their recent visit were both informative and entertaining. Several slides really excited James. He nudged me and whispered.

"Look, that was my school district."

"See that road, I walked down it for many miles every day to go to school."

"And there's that sign in the village saying this is the line of the equator that the tourists always stop to take pictures of, but I don't believe the location is very accurate."

After the slide show, the presenter asked a member of the audience to come up and say a few words. Much to James' surprise it turned out to be his close Kenyan friend, Mr. Ngongo, a tall, elegant handsome man wearing a colourful African shirt. He presented his personal story with quiet but strong resolve. After his talk, much to our surprise, Bill pointed to James and asked him to also come up and say a few words. Even more to my surprise, James agreed. Both speeches were unbelievably moving. Ten-year veterans of Toastmasters International had nothing on these guys. Many of the audience, including myself, were tamping the tears from their eyes.

I joked with James afterwards. "Where did you guys learn to speak like that?"

"Simple... we just say what our heart tells us."

The message from the evening clearly reinforced my resolve for action to work to help advance education in impoverished areas.

Both James and Mr. Ngongo, by managing to educate themselves through to university level despite their impoverished beginnings, were excellent examples of a dogged determination to succeed.

I also started thinking about formalizing my commitment to this new career in the form of a charitable organization. I was willing to personally finance these first two schools, but if I were to build more, as much as I dislike bureaucracy I would need to form a charitable organization in order to get donations from others. I spent every spare hour researching the structure and running of a charity, how to apply, and how to get approval of charity status in the shortest time.

My research led me to a Vancouver lawyer, Margaret Mason, who specializes in charity applications, and typically can get approval in four to five months – half of the usual time. Through her office, we completed the required steps; first, the registration of our name, then the incorporation as a society, *Primary Schools For Africa Society*, and then the application to Revenue Canada for charity status. It would be a nervous wait, but I felt confident of success. Meanwhile, I would focus all my energy on these two school projects. They would have to be successful; the credibility of the future charity hinged on it.

James and I finalized the construction documents; I sent them to

Jacob and Mathew for review, and then made a few subsequent revisions to everyone's satisfaction. The process of starting construction was coming together reasonably well. I could monitor the first few stages of construction from Victoria. Mathew and Jacob would inspect the quality of work and send photos for verification, and I would then forward progress payments. My plan was to go there for only the final two to three weeks of the projects.

However, with the construction start date looming, I began to feel anxious about the reliability of money transfers from Canada to Arusha. I had forwarded Cdn$15,000 to be used as progress payments, but after four days, with no confirmation of its arrival into my new Arusha account, I decided this would have to be a hands-on project, from start to finish. Within two days, I had my flight booked. I stuffed the remaining amount needed for the schools, Cdn$24,000, in the pockets of my cargo pants and was on my way to Africa.

CHAPTER 3

CLAY, STONES, CONCRETE

"Teamwork divides the task and multiplies the success."

— AUTHOR UNKNOWN

Concrete for post footing. Note the hand-broken rock sub-base.

At 10:00PM on November 7, Mathew picked me up at Kilimanjaro Airport. Despite my exhaustion from the 22-hour flight, I enjoyed our lively friendly discussion in the back of an old run-down taxicab on the one-hour ride to my rustic accommodations in Arusha, the Outpost Lodge. Mathew was relieved to see me, as our construction schedule was a key issue: the rainy season usually begins around mid-November. It was Sunday November 7th, so things had to move quickly or we'd be pouring concrete floors in the rain.

First thing Monday morning, Mathew phoned. He suggested accompanying me and insisted on taking a taxi to the bank, where we were both relieved to unload the cash. After withdrawing start-up bundles of Tanzanian shillings for both projects, we quickly strolled the streets, looking for a good coffee shop, as excited as a couple of kids leaving a candy shop with pockets full of sweet treats, anxious to discuss the details of our new adventure.

It was a pleasantly warm day. The weather had cooled a little since my September visit, but this region, at 4,000 to 5,000 feet above sea level, never really gets too hot, with year-round temperatures varying between 77 to 86°F. The colourful hustle and bustle of Arusha's city centre matched my mood; after a good night's sleep, I was energized and anxious to met the builders and discuss the projects. Mathew ushered me into a seat in a popular and crowded coffee shop, and returned a little later, proudly smiling, with a couple of steaming mugs of excellent local java, grown locally on the slopes of Kilimanjaro. As I was laying out the drawings, ready to discuss the school design, his mood darkened a little.

"I am sad today," he said.

I was perplexed by his unexpected change of mood. "Uh-oh, bad news about the project?"

"No, no," he reassured. "I am sorry… it is still fresh in our minds; our national election on October 31 last week was unsuccessful for our candidate, Dr. Willibrod Peter Slaa, the leader of our *Chama Cha Demokrasia* (Party For Democracy). President Jakaya Kikwete was re-elected, but the people are not happy. We believe the counting of the ballots was false. We should have received more than 27 per cent of the vote."

I remembered the election fever back in September, when posters of Kikwete were plastered on every spare building wall space, and pickup trucks cruised the streets, with their roof-mounted loudspeakers blaring political slogans, and their cargo areas housing makeshift trumpet bands deliriously blasting out brass cacophonies. I noticed how indifferent the public appeared; it belied the blatant attempt at showing support and confidence in the incumbent.

"What makes you believe the ballot count was rigged?" I asked.

"Simple – the existing government offices controlled the ballot counting. We have no way of verifying the real numbers."

Sighing, and then with a fierce look, he said, "But let's forget about that; now we have a school to build. We will leave for Gongali tomorrow. Philemon, the village mayor, has already arranged to have a ceremony to officially start construction."

Mathew's eyes lit up. "And there is great news; Lazarus Titus will also be there," he continued. "Fortunately for us, he was re-elected as chairman of our Manyara district in the election last week. Both Dr. Slaa and Mr. Titus believe that education is important for the growth of our region and our country. Mr. Titus had been made aware of our school project and wishes to show his appreciation by personally meeting you to offer the full support of his office."

"Wonderful," I said. "We need as much government awareness as possible to make our future projects easier."

I thought to myself that there might be an opportunity with Mr. Titus as someone who could help us register our charity as an official NGO [non-government organization].

We were huddling over the design drawings when Mathew interrupted. "We have something to admit, Alan. Fabian and I did not understand some of your drawing. Can you explain what that is?" he said, pointing to the building section, and some connection details.

I realized then that, though these drawings were only a fraction of the complexity I was used to in western construction documentation, they could overwhelm a village contractor who would normally rely on nothing more than a hand-drawn sketch, or an image scratched out on a piece of wood, or simply a memorized conversation.

"I hope Fabian's price is reliable," I said nervously. "His material list seemed complete enough." I paused. "Mathew, what do you think? Is he going to work out?"

"Hakuna matata, Alan. He has built several buildings in our village, and he has friends to do the carpentry and the concrete work who are very experienced. They have worked on another school project in our region."

"Good. Well, when we meet with him, we'll go over the plans in detail. I'm looking forward to a good relationship where we can learn from each other."

✏️

Later that afternoon, back at the lodge, I contacted an enthusiastic Jacob who insisted on bringing Hemedi Iddi, our Majengo builder, to the lodge to meet me. I was introduced to a middle-aged man, quiet and soft-spoken, and even a little shy at first, but who later confirmed in my mind, a confidence drawn from many years of experience.

Since Hemedi spoke no English, Jacob translated our conversation.

"Are you OK with the design and the drawings?" I asked.

Hemedi simply nodded his head.

That was my cue to hand over the first payment. "Then when can we start?"

"Tomorrow," he replied.

✏️

Tuesday's visit to the Gongali site was very eventful. Mathew had arranged for his friend George to drive us there in his road-weary

Hemedi (left), Jacob, Alan – getting to know each other at first meeting.

1978 Toyota. It seemed to be on its last legs; the electric windows didn't work, the tires were balding, and the incessant car-rattling was nerve-rattling. The ride consisted of the usual bumps on the stretch of paved road from Arusha to the Lake Manyara junction. From that junction to Karatu, and onwards to the Serengeti Plains, runs a comfortable, newly-paved highway, built with funds donated by the Japanese government, complete with "modern" roadside washroom facilities. For future reference I took note of the construction, in particular, the concrete septic tank design. Interestingly, on this trip, we were not treated to any roadside wildlife.

When we arrived at the village we went directly to the site.

Two dozen or so villagers formed a semi-circle around several important individuals who stood in the middle of a cleared section of the pigeon pea crop field. On the way to the site, I had been looking forward to some lively discussions regarding where on the large treeless 10-acre field we would locate the building. As it turned out, I didn't have too much say in the matter; Philemon, the mayor, and Fabian, the builder, had previously instructed villagers to clear the crops in an area they felt was suitable. It seemed a little arbitrary, but I trusted that their decision was probably based on local knowledge of wind and sun factors.

I recognized Peter Hayshi, the district vice-chairman, but not the tall elegant well-dressed man in the centre. Mathew's excitement to introduce me reflected his respect for this man. He grabbed my hand and led me to Lazarus Titus, the district chairman, who was more than happy to dignify the official groundbreaking ceremony. He greeted me warmly and I immediately sensed the generous and compassionate nature that made him so well respected in the district, qualities that had led to his recent re-election.

Mathew then introduced me to Fabian and a few of his smiling workers. To my surprise, he was only about 25 to 27 years old, thin but muscular. Like Hemedi, Fabian was soft-spoken and could speak no English. His youthful enthusiasm and broad gleaming smile, however, made me feel optimistic about our working together successfully.

To the loud cheers and clapping of the villagers, Lazarus and I struck the dusty red clay soil with crude hoes.

Fabian then proceeded to lay out the building perimeter with string lines in the approximate centre of the clearing. He placed a peg at the starting corner and connected a home-made measuring tape to it, then proceeded tentatively to the next corner.

Piles of stone for the foundations were already placed off to the side of the building. Many villagers from nearby farms had scoured their fields to collect the large rocks. As we pegged out the lines, a truck drove up filled with more workers than stones.

The atmosphere was filled with joyous activity, with strapping young workmen laughing and joking with each other and forming groups that took turns off-loading the large boulders.

This was an unusual event for the dignitaries, who seemed a little at a loss with what to do at the site. Excitement underlined the behavior of Mathew, Peter and Lazarus, as they followed Fabian's every move. They wanted to be involved (*client participation – a builder's worst nightmare*, I thought).

As they discussed the dimensions needed for the classrooms, my first thought was, "Where are the plans?"

Nowhere in sight. In fact, not even on site. I asked Mathew to question Fabian. I wasn't surprised with Fabian's response, which was that he had memorized the dimensions – easy enough with such a simple building. Or was it?

The discussions became more animated; there was some confusion about the length of the building. I had been busy videotaping the events with my camera, but was called over to the group to settle the "argument."

"Babu Alan," Mathew asked, "what is the width of the breeze-way, and where is it located?"

We were gathered around Fabian's homemade tape measure and I noticed that it was marked out in one-foot increments. Just then it dawned on me that the probable reason for the "mislaid" plans was that I had shown the dimensions in metric. I couldn't transpose exactly to imperial quickly enough so I rounded off the dimensions: "You come thirty feet this way for the first classroom, then five feet for the breezeway, then another thirty feet for the second classroom."

We then pegged out the length of the building, with the breeze-way positioned at the halfway point between the classrooms.

This event spurred an important realization; the communication of the design had to be simplest in the utmost. It soon became evident that the plan details were probably quite foreign to Fabian; he had never seen a proper set of working drawings, and given the simplicity of the structure, perhaps felt they were not necessary.

The site visit lasted only a few hours. I wanted to roll up my sleeves and work with Fabian on the layout, but it was important to have project discussions with Lazarus Titus and his associates while I had the opportunity. In any case, Mayor Philemon had other plans for me, and suggested we leave. But before I left, Mathew and I met with Fabian and went over the layout using a folded drawing I had in my back pocket.

My impression of Fabian was one of quiet intelligence; he was soft spoken, in fact he spoke only rarely, and I wondered whether it was because of a total understanding, or an inherent shyness. Mathew assured me that he fully understood the information, but I was not convinced. I would later have my doubts confirmed.

The "dignitaries" and I proceeded to a lunch arranged by Mayor Philemon at the home of one of the villagers. It was located in the middle of a rectangular compound surrounded by tightly spaced *minyaa* trees. It reminded me of Maureen's family farm in Manitoba, where for the same reason, lines of trees planted by farmers provided windbreak protection from the harsh winter winds that could quickly build up snow against farm buildings and homes. Here, it was to keep down the wind-driven fine red dust.

The home was one of the better-built structures in the village, but sadly, the only opening admitting daylight to the main room where we ate was the entranceway, which had no actual door. It was interesting to experience the gradual appearances of everyone in the room as our eyes acclimatized to the dark interior. As we feasted on chicken stew with copious amounts of rice, Peter Hayshi confirmed the total co-operation of his office. School registration, teachers, school supplies and all post-construction issues would be well taken care of.

Our driver, George, drove Mathew and me through the maze of car-rattling, bumpy and dusty village trails back to Karatu where Mathew had decided to stay overnight so he could help his sister support their convalescing mother who was recovering from her recent operation.

George and I then left for Arusha around 5:00PM. I was exhausted from the day's activities, so I tilted the passenger seat as far back as it would go and instantly fell asleep.

An explosion woke me up, catapulting me forward into the dashboard, and causing the car to swerve quickly into the shoulder of the road.

"George, what the hell was that?" I shouted.

"We hit pothole. Couldn't avoid. There was truck in other lane."

We hobbled to a stop, got out and assessed the damage. It was pitch black.

"Where are we?" I asked. "How far from Arusha?"

"Maybe 10 or 15 miles," George said.

I must have been asleep for at least an hour and a half; I didn't realize how close we were to Arusha.

"This is not good place to stop," George continued. "Many bad people who rob you on this part of road."

As George explained, the west side of Arusha is rampant with cruising young criminally-minded opportunists. Needless to say, I got a little anxious.

The rear tire was shredded and the shock absorber (a piston rod that slides up and down inside a fluid-filled cylinder surrounded by a coil ring) was broken. The piston rod, under the force of the impact, had broken in half. The freely hinged lower part had then jammed itself into the tire, causing the explosion.

I abandoned any notion of trying to fix what seemed to be an insurmountable problem.

"Let's phone a tow truck," I suggested.

I didn't quite understand his rationale, but his body language convinced me that would be too difficult.

"I will fix," he said. After looking into the wheel well cavity for a few minutes, he announced he had a plan. But he did look a little worried.

Thank God for cell phones which can be used as flashlights. With them stuck in our mouths, we scoured the flat Maasai fields for large rocks of various thicknesses and piled them up alongside the car. The rear side of the car had to be jacked up beyond the range of the jack, not only to remove the tire but to remove the coil ring and somehow jam the lower piston into a (conveniently-located) slotted groove in the car's underbody. We would raise the car to the full extent of the jack, then insert rocks under the rocker panel, lower the car to settle on the rocks, insert a smaller flat rock under the jack to be able to raise the car even further, and so on until we reached the desired height. The car collapsed and crashed to the ground at the first attempt. We were so tired we forgot to chock the wheels with stones to prevent the car from rolling.

Just then, a car pulled over and stopped behind us. The radio was cranked up. Three young men got out and slowly walked over to us. Much to my relief, they were not even interested in our plight. They had problems of their own; a flat tire; and could they borrow our jack? ("Yes, but you have to wait your turn," I mused.)

At the second attempt, the car was high enough to jam the piston rod into the slot. George replaced the tire with his very bald spare. Then we very carefully maneuvered ourselves to Arusha no faster than a bicycle, with the vehicle's rear end amusingly tilted high above the rest of the car. It was working, but with no rear shock we felt every little bump in the road. Two hours later, totally exhausted, we made it to the Outpost Lodge.

"Thanks, George, you were amazing."

"Hakuna matata. Good night and sleep well."

While undressing for bed, I noticed my reading glasses were missing from my shirt pocket; probably somewhere out on that vast Maasai landscape.

᠅

On Wednesday afternoon I met Jacob Slaa and Hemedi the builder at the Majengo site. I was surprised to see all of the trenching dug out for the foundations stones. Labour here is incredibly cheap; a few dollars a day for an unskilled worker. Teddy and Cosmas were anxiously awaiting my arrival and greeted me with such warmth.

"Karibu sana [very welcome], Babu Alan, karibu sana."

"Babu Mkubwa [Grandfather Senior] Alan," I jokingly corrected (referring to my Kilimanjaro climb title bestowed by the porters). We laughed.

Jacob's translation of Teddy continued, "Welcome back to Tanzania and to our Majengo village. We did not know if you would return until Jacob told us that we now have a builder for the school. That made everyone in the village excited and very happy.

Since then, everyone, especially the excited orphan children, have been asking me every day; when will the school be finished?"

"I plan to be here only five weeks. My hope is that it will be complete by then." An ambitious hope, I thought. It would really depend on how committed the workers felt.

So far, I was suitably impressed. I waved to the builder Hemedi, who was expertly orchestrating the frenzied work of a half-dozen or so young men. He looked like he had everything under control. It confirmed my confidence in his ability. We discussed a few details and procedures and then retired into Teddy's small living room to formally sign the contract.

On the way back to the lodge, I mused how all this was all happening so quickly, and so smoothly. But as it happened, thanks to "Mr. Murphy", there would be a few serious wrinkles.

⁑

Thursday, the 11th of November, was a day of rest and reflection. It was Remembrance Day back home; I thought about my uncle "Mac" who was killed in Italy during World War II trying to break through the famed Nazi Gustav line between Rome and Cortona. He was a young, 27-year-old infantryman, serving under the command of an even younger Lieutenant named Farley Mowat, the now renowned writer and poet. I felt an interesting connection; Mac and I were the only ones in our recent family generations to have been that far away from home; his battle was tyranny, mine was illiteracy.

I also reflected on the lifelong humanitarian work in Africa accomplished by my Victoria friends Don Hatfield and his wife Sylvia over a period of 35 years, for which they received the Order of Canada. Don is a former military chaplain who was stationed in North Africa. He is also the presiding chaplain for one of the Remembrance Day ceremonies held every year in Victoria. Always elegant and thoughtful, his service on that Thursday was the first one I had missed in 14 years. Sylvia is an extraordinary woman with boundless energy who founded a charity, *Canada Comforts*, that employs an army of volunteer women all across Canada who craft fabric toys and clothing for African children.

On Friday, I met with a lawyer, Mr. Marcellino Mwamnyange, at the Arusha office of the Attorney General Department. He was the same lawyer who had provided a letter of reference for me that was needed to open a bank account. I had known him for less than five minutes, but for forty dollars, he verified my "vertical" status: "I have known him for a while having introduced himself as a volunteer and I believe he is an upright person".

I was now anxious to register in Tanzania as an NGO. As Mathew later explained, this lawyer happened to be the son of the famous General Mwamnyange of the Tanzanian Army. Marcellino was a very small man, well-dressed, and with a shy but friendly nature. After explaining to him my intentions, he gave me the list of needed documentation. I would need to forward it to him when I returned to Canada. He would then walk the application through the various levels of government bureaucracy, including a personal visit to the capital city of Dar Es Salaam. His fees?

"Maybe you could arrange to send me a good American computer?"

I didn't know what to make of it.

"New or used, it doesn't matter," he continued. "I am a very busy prosecutor. I go to court every afternoon and must carry many reference books of law."

He described his frustration with the lack of speedy reference material during trials.

"When I must prove my point, I waste a lot of time leafing through my many books. A laptop computer would be most helpful, but I cannot afford one on my modest salary."

I agreed to get him one.

Later that morning, George drove Mathew and me to Gongali for site visit number two. He had wasted little time repairing the car with a new shock absorber.

On the way, George pointed out the spot where we had broken down three nights before.

"Stop here for a minute," I quickly blurted. "I think I dropped my glasses here the other night."

We couldn't find them. George explained that the Maasai children walk many miles along the road every day to go to school. Hopefully, the glasses are now being well used by some other Babu.

I enjoyed the now familiar drive – starting with the flat plains, treeless, except for the few small surviving bonsai-like shrubs and thorn bushes, populated sparsely with Maasai men who seemed to aimlessly herd their cattle, searching for what little grass was available on the barren gravelled landscape; and after reaching Lake Manyara, the tight S-turns climb through the more densely shrubbed hills overlooking the lake; and finally, through the upper plateau region of the Karatu district through the Maasai tourist village of Mto Wa Mbu (Mosquito Creek), where the bright colours of the Maasai paintings that endlessly lined up along both sides of the road were outdone only by the magnificence of the occasional bright red *delonix regia* "Flaming Tree".

The wildlife treat of the day: passing through a herd of fifteen to twenty elephants strolling along both sides of the road near Mosquito Creek. I also noticed that "stray baboons," who were looking for easy food, similar to our "citified" deer and bear in British Columbia towns, seemed to be an integral part of the local population.

As we passed the village and neared the school site, George's car broke down. This time it was the fuel pump. We abandoned the car and hiked the last few miles.

At the site, builder Fabian and his crew of about fifteen villagers were making good progress with the foundations. Shallow trenches had been dug from the stiff red clay soil along string lines that formed the rectangular perimeter of the building. The trenches had been filled with stones broken into irregular shaped pieces, except at the corners and at wall junctions, where four vertical steel rebar rods would be set in the concrete. The rods would rigidly reinforce the concrete columns to the floor.

My heart sank. I noticed that the building looked a little "out of square". We checked the diagonal dimensions, and sure enough, they didn't match; not even close. His rectangle was actually a parallelogram. Through Mathew's translation, Fabian explained that he had basically just "eyeballed" it with the help of a little 6-inch x 8-inch square placed at each corner. Fabian looked sad and did not seem to have a solution. At first I have to admit I was a little disappointed with the apparent lack of expertise. When I was in Canada, I had asked Mathew to find a good builder, and in all

Determining the layout error of the foundation at the Gongali site.

fairness to him, he did comply. Fabian was considered one of the best local builders (in the village), but his experience was limited to a few small houses. This incident was fully understandable; our technologies were worlds apart, and as I had anticipated, it would be a process of continual learning from each other.

However, the distorted layout was a major issue that could create problems with the installation of ceiling and roof sheeting, so it had to be fixed. The workers stopped when they sensed something was amiss and watched quietly as I stood staring at the corner of the string lines, contemplating the next move. I was saddened by the thought of the extra work it would take for them to re-excavate the trenches and move the stones over.

How were we going to fix this? I finally broke the silence: "Fabian, Mathew, please find me two 6- or 8-feet-long pieces of lumber."

I instructed them to bring them to one corner. I nailed the corners of the two six foot lengths of lumber to create a hinged joint and marked out 48 inches along each piece. Fortunately, I had brought my calculator and, using Pythagoras' Theorem – which is simple geometry for calculating the unknown dimension of a right-angled triangle, that Canadian kids learn in Grade 8 – I calculated the diagonal's dimension to be 68 inches. We then constructed the large set-square and placed it at the corner. Three villagers held it firmly in place while others realigned and re-pegged the string lines parallel to the edges of the lumber. This process was repeated at each corner until we arrived at a perfect rectangle. The diagonal measurements of the rectangle should then be the same. We measured and they checked out within an inch – good enough!

Fabian looked at me, and with a huge smile, thanked me with a few Swahili words. Mathew explained that he was extremely pleased to have learned a new "trick." I imagined him now happily lugging around as a part of his standard tool kit, this large 48-inch x 48-inch x 68-inch set-square.

I asked Mathew if he or the villagers were disappointed with having to do most of the work all over again.

"On the contrary, they are very pleased to have a better school now."

Layout error correction with the new "set-square".

The villagers went back to work with seemingly renewed vigor. Thank God for that.

Fabian and Philemon had prepared a list of materials and their cost for the next batch of supplies. I reviewed it and after discussing it and agreeing on some details of the next phase of work, Mathew and I agreed it was late and we should head back to Arusha now to avoid night-time travel.

George was successful in replacing the fuel pump. He managed to get a ride back to Karatu where he picked up a used one, and got back to the vehicle to do the repairs. But getting into the old Toyota, I happened to notice that although the shock absorber was new, the replacement tire on the rear wheel was very bald. I was worrying about a blowout any minute on the rough stretches of road, which made for an uneasy ride back. However this time we made it without incident.

It was another long Gongali project day; I slept well that night.

❧

Saturday, November 13, was a day of rest and writing.

At the Majengo school site on Sunday afternoon, I was pleasantly surprised to see how much progress had been made since the first visit. Jacob, builder Hemedi, Teddy and Cosmas greeted me with their usual cheery, "Karibu sana, karibu sana."

The foundation walls built out of two rows of block were done up to the underside of the floor level. Several workers were shoveling the clay subsoil into the areas in between the walls. The filled areas were being compacted by soaking them with water. A heavyset "traditionally-built" woman was carrying water one bucket at a time from a 45-gallon drum located some distance down the road. There was city water piped in trickling amounts to the site, but it was not working for some reason.

Once the clay subfloor compaction was finished, all that would remain would be a layer of compacted gravel, then the wire mesh, and then the hand mixing of concrete for the floor.

I decided to check a few dimensions, just to be safe. And again, my heart would sink. Unfortunately, the length of the building was a foot short from the design. Hemedi couldn't believe it, but after checking it himself he verified the error. He seemed a little ashamed, so I assured him that "these things happen", and he still had my confidence.

As I reflected on whether it would really matter to the layout, he quickly offered; "No problem, I will fix."

He would dig out the extra trenching and extend the foundation wall without requiring further discussion (and, to my relief, any further cost).

I then asked Jacob to sit with Teddy, Cosmas and me to have an important discussion. I explained to them how concerned I was with the state of the plumbing facilities in their home. At my last visit, I discovered that their only toilet – which was shared by themselves, the several single mothers and their children on the property – was a hole in the floor in an attached shed against the end of their house. The below floor septic design was nothing more than that of a latrine. Also, there wasn't a sink anywhere on the property; they used a tap on a pipe sticking out of the ground next to the house. I couldn't imagine the difficulties they must be having with their daily routine, in and out of the house, at all times of the day and night, in all kinds of weather. How did they prepare meals without adjacent water? I thought of the wonderful gourmet meals my wife Maureen could whip up at a moment's notice, and how silly we were to sometimes struggle for the space in front of the sink when preparing meals together.

I thought about their situation for the next few days. I was upset that a woman of Teddy's stature in the community was living like this. I admired and respected the selfless work she did for her community; there must be something I could do. I considered the obvious solution: building an extension to her house to replace the shed. However, after a few quick calculations, I realized it would mean exhausting my limited contingency funds.

In the morning before the Majengo site visit, I had another idea. I would alter the design of the school to add a shower room that could be shared by all. It would be in a separate room alongside the enclosed toilet room. A sink would be located in a common area adjacent to both rooms. This arrangement would provide the most flexibility of use by both residents and pupils.

I presented my quick sketch of the new layout to Teddy and Cosmas. Jacob explained what I was up to and translated their reaction. I could see for myself from their surprise and grins that they were delighted. I sensed they were also overwhelmed by the thought of such a life-changing turn of events.

We then met with Hemedi to get his reaction and cost estimate for the additional work involved. Changes are usually a contractor's worst nightmare after construction is started. I was pleased that he was very positive and accommodating. He would get back to me in 24 hours with a price and any scheduling issues.

✸

Monday was an administrative day for Jacob and me. First stop, the bank, to get progress payment number two for Jacob and three for Mathew.

We elected to make all our financial transactions in cash, as cheques were impractical and unreliable. Considering the short construction timetable, the builders benefited from the speediness of cash to purchase materials and make payments to subcontractors.

Similar to previous visits, we were again invited to the second floor offices of the bank manager, Maternus Malibishe and his staff, Godwin Elisa and Shabami Mbegu. Mr. Malibiche was a rotund, somewhat serious, but very accommodating man, who, during introductions, emphasized his name proudly, with resounding resonance. The preferential treatment I guessed was due to our charity work. I was not complaining, having been spared the long waits in the cashier line-ups. He left and returned within five minutes with the total of over 13 million shillings (Cdn$9,200). The size of the bundle of cash was surprising; in maximum 10,000 shillings bills, it amounted to 8 inches thick.

Normally, I carry the money and personally deliver it to the builders, but I wasn't going to the site that day, so I handed Jacob his project's share. He then went behind an empty desk, sat down and bent forward.

"What are you doing," I asked as he was rolling up his pantlegs.

"I have my special Kilimanjaro socks on today," as he proceeded to stuff the cash in equal-sized bundles of shilling bills in his new wool socks. "This is my trick."

Jacob explained that although most of his travel was by taxi, there were short walking distances when he and Hemedi visited suppliers in the crowded rundown commercial areas of Majengo, and therefore it was important to be as inconspicuous as possible. He assured me that the money would get distributed as quickly as possible during the day since there was no safe and practical way to store it overnight. The precautions made sense, and also made me think twice about loading up my briefcase during my site visits.

Jacob and I were enjoying working together, and he was more than happy to be learning construction administration procedures. We were amassing enough paperwork now from the progress claims and our first Change Order (contract price change) that I felt it was time to supply him with some office basics: a binder, section dividers with tabs, a two-hole punch and a stapler. He was extremely pleased. Believe it or not, he had never had such basic supplies. This surprised me, as he was a former teacher. It was another reminder how poorly-equipped schools are in this country.

≯⅄ϟ

On Tuesday, 16 November, it was back to Gongali for visit number three.

I had talked to Mathew about his friend George and his Toyota mishaps. In light of the car's memorable adventures, we agreed that it was time to look for more reliable transportation. With the rains now a little more frequent, we began to worry more about whether we would make it to our destination or not.

Deogratius (nicknamed Deo) Augustino Mpogole was one of the Outpost Lodge regulars. He and several other taxi drivers "owned" the turf in front of the lodge, and made themselves available at a moment's notice to the guests. He was my regular for the occasional trips to the bank and to the Majengo site; a short, stocky, good-natured Tanzanian whose hearty laugh could be heard from every corner of the lodge property. In his mid-forties, he had just started wearing glasses, and was still a little uncomfortable with them. We chatted regularly, particularly in the early mornings when I did my regular one-hour walk around the neighbourhood. He was a family man, who frequently phoned to chat with his wife, even while driving during his runs.

"How are Magdelena and the girls doing," I would ask.

"Hakuna matata, Babu Alan. Elisa and Eloise are doing fine at primary school, but Lucy is struggling with a career choice in Form 5 [equivalent to our Grade 12]."

"Your girls' names are very similar," I noted.

"Yes, my wife likes the letter L."

Deo is one of the more fastidious car owners. He has a newer (only 15 years old) Toyota Corolla; the tires are good, the windows are operable, and the windshield wipers work. He keeps his car spotlessly clean, inside and out, and can frequently be seen wiping off raindrops or dust between runs. This car is his life, his pride and joy.

We offered him the Gongali trip. He was very pleased to be hired for the day. With a daily average of only five or six runs, at about 3,000 shillings per run, this 140,000 shillings (Cdn$100) assignment would pay him more than two week's income. He may not have been so grateful if he knew what was in store for him.

Deo and I had an early start. We left the Outpost at 6:00AM and picked up Mathew at his home on the way out of town. It had poured rain all night, but thankfully precipitation had reduced to a light rain by morning. The temperature was a little cool, maybe 64°F. I was surprised how warmly dressed Deo and Mathew were, with their toques and lined winter jackets. Mathew was wearing his well-loved suede jacket. I had only my thin shell jacket over my shirt. The "cold" affects Tanzanians much more than I had expected.

We arrived in Karatu by 9:00AM. Mathew had arranged for us to meet Mayor Philemon at a local restaurant for a quick breakfast meeting. Most local restaurants in Karatu have open air tables under makeshift roofs of sheet metal supported by flimsily constructed wood rafters and posts made from the local *minyaa* trees. However, this restaurant was considered one of the town's finest. It had an exceptional feature; its tables were located inside small circular thatched roof huts measuring not more than seven feet across, one table per hut. Very charming idea, except that when it rained, as it did that day, the servers got wet going from hut to hut. It didn't seem to bother them though.

Philemon hadn't shown up yet. Mathew and Deo were hungry so we decided to go ahead with an order. I just wanted toast and coffee. Mathew called the manager over.

"What? You only have chicken soup and coffee? You have no eggs? Or milk? How can you not have bread, the bakery has been open for hours?"

"We never have much business this early..."

Before he could finish, Mathew pulled out a few bills and sent him off to buy "supplies". He returned a few moments later with eggs, bread, milk and for Mathew's favourite on toast, a jar of pineapple jam.

After ten or fifteen minutes, Mathew decided to phone Philemon. He reported, "Philemon's motorcycle is stuck in the sticky clay mud on the Gongali road. He is walking. Maybe someone will pick him up."

When Philemon finally arrived on the back of a neighbour's

motorcycle, wet and anxious, he wanted to quickly get down to business.

"The supplies of cement and wire mesh for the floor are loaded up on the truck and are waiting at Marco's store. Marco won't release the driver until he gets paid."

Marco's, by the way, is the main centre for builder's supplies in Karatu. When I was here in September, pricing his material, we asked Marco to "donate" a discount for the school project. No way!

"This is probably why he is so rich," Philemon explained.

I was happy to hand over the bundle of cash to Philemon for Fabian's progress payment. After quickly stuffing it inside his shirt, and making sure the coast was clear, he left us, not interested in joining us to finish our breakfast.

On the way out, Mathew had another interesting conversation with the manager.

"What was that all about?" I asked.

"I told her to keep my jar of jam until my next visit."

"And will she?"

"Yes, I trust them, they are very honorable here."

Her compliance was probably more due to Mathew's charm and likeability.

The day's adventure started the moment we left the paved road at Karatu and headed south to the village. The normally fine, red dusty dirt roads were now muddy and barely navigable unless you were in a four-wheel-drive. It was about two miles to the village and another four to the school site. We crawled no faster than walking speed, regularly getting bogged down to a standstill. When we got stuck, Deo would gun the engine sending clay mud flying out from beneath the wheels. By "rocking" the car in and out of forward and reverse, we would eventually get out. To make things worse, the lower level of the car in the mud made the large stones in the road more prominent. *Bang! Scrrrrrape!* The undercarriage was taking a beating. Several large trucks passed, splashing mud over the car's windows.

Deo's cheery disposition had evaporated. His jaw muscles were working overtime. He was perspiring and his glasses were fogging up. Just past the village the road was now becoming impassible. Mathew grew up in this area, and suggested we turn off of the road to get on a tractor path crossing a field as a short cut to the site. We got out to survey it and after stamping it with our muddy feet, we determined it was hard enough. But it was a bad decision. There was a ditch between us and the field that seemed passable enough, rolling down gently and up onto the field. When Deo accelerated to angle over the hump, the car got hung up diagonally on two wheels. The forward in-gear wheel was freely spinning in the air, and the lower rear one was jammed into the thick clay mud.

It was raining hard now. I felt sorry for Deo, who got out and circled around his beloved but now despoiled chariot, hoping for a way out of this mess. To add insult to injury, when he bent over, his glasses fell off into the mud. He picked them up and without cleaning them off, angrily threw them into the car. He was clearly disparaged, not only with the mud and possible damage to the undercarriage, but with his failure to get us to the site.

Mathew and I abandoned the car to hoof out the last couple of miles. Deo elected to stay and pray for some passing help.

When the school construction appeared in the distance, I could see good progress. The subfloor of rocks and sand was completed, ready for the hand mixing of the concrete. Concrete footings with vertical rebar extensions were in place at the column locations. The only thing awry was that no one was working, and it wasn't due to the rain. The first truckload of materials, bags of cement and wire mesh for the floor, had not yet arrived. The fifteen or so workers were huddled inside a small temporary storage building that Fabian had constructed out of lumber and sheet metal roofing that would eventually be used for the roof. They needed it to keep the bags of cement from getting wet. Good planning!

Mathew, Fabian and I scanned the horizon for some sign of movement. Mathew kept phoning Philemon who was with the driver for progress reports on the truck's progress. It was inching along like we had been. And sure enough, as Mathew reported, it had finally bogged down. It had attempted the short cut across the same field as us and had made it up over the hump, but only to be mired in a soft patch of the field.

"Would it help," I suggested, "if we all went to lend a hand? Maybe we could unload and carry the supplies... somehow."

"What else can we do?" agreed Mathew and Fabian.

It was still raining hard. As we hiked across the countryside, I asked Mathew why all the workers were chattering so excitedly.

"Some say the driver doesn't know how to use gears. Another says he has taken too much load. They laugh when someone says he should go back to driving tractor."

I was amazed at the frenzy of activity when we got to the truck. These guys had experience; getting stuck was a regular thing during the rainy season. With a couple of large hoes, they took turns digging a long channel, about eight inches deep and twenty feet long, along the line of each wheel, to get down to hard clay.

Mathew even threw himself into the effort. He took off his suede jacket and throwing it on the ground, went to work like a whirling dervish. Within minutes, the driver was ready for his attempt. With everyone jammed up at the truck's backside to push, he gunned it, accelerating slowly, and to the cheers of the men, was finally able to get up enough speed to climb out of the ruts and be on his way. And then more laughter – at the comical look of several men who were covered in mud sprayed from the spinning tires.

Back at the site, with everything off-loaded, some workers quickly mixed sand, cement, gravel and water while others placed sheets of wire mesh to reinforce the floor slab. In an adjacent area, a large circular ring of sand was prepared, with sloped sides to contain the ingredients. Then buckets of sand and gravel were added along with the bags of cement. Finally, water was hosed from a 1500-litre [330-gallon] plastic tank (our future elevated water supply) in gradual amounts while several workers with shovels turned over the mixture until it attained an even texture.

I was a little anxious about whether or not they were mixing the correct proportion of ingredients. Fabian assured me that that little fellow, the "counter," sitting on the pile of gravel with his cell phone, was in control. He was punching in numbers, displayed in sequence, to ensure the correct buckets of sand and gravel were being heaved into the mix along with each bag of cement. I was impressed; it was an ingenious and resourceful use of a simple and available technology.

From the mixing area, teams of workers carried buckets of concrete to the foundations and then spread the mixture evenly across the floor area. I joined in the effort for a couple of hours or so. It was back-straining work.

By late morning, a smiling Deo had arrived at the site. A local tractor driver had pulled him out and onto the field and he'd been able to manage the rest. As it turned out, the weather would soon clear and by late afternoon the roads would be sufficiently dried-out to be drive-able. Deo normally spends most of his day back in Arusha waiting for fares, but at the site, he found himself eager to learn construction. At every opportunity that arose, he volunteered to help wherever he could, performing small tasks that he carried out with unprecedented energy.

Around midday, several village women arrived and cooked the workers' staple: *ugali*, ground white corn boiled in a large pot of water, gelled to a custard-like consistency. Slabs were ripped off, then heartily eaten with fingers. I enjoyed some; it tasted a bit like rice.

After lunch, I was delighted and surprised when I peered into the storage shed to witness some construction. To animated discussion, a few men were building a present for me: a desk and bench, with hand-sawn planks of wood left over from the formwork.

"This is now your office," they said. "You must have desk and chair."

"Ahsante, Ahsante [thank you]," I gushed, while exchanging hearty Tanzanian handshakes. Another moment to remember and cherish.

Mathew and I spent the following hour discussing the upcoming stages of work. Next would be the masonry walls. Then concrete posts and lintel beams would be formed using the walls to support the wood forms. When finished, since the blocks are "non structural," the posts and lintel beams would contain the walls, effectively holding them in place. It was the standard construction for small buildings seen everywhere. Structurally, this is very ingenious, and somewhat the reverse of our western method of building the "posts" into the walls using hollow blocks to allow the installation of reinforcing rods and cement.

I discussed roof-framing details at length with Fabian. His method of tying down the roof rafters to the lintel beams with pieces of wire installed in the lintel concrete seemed a little iffy. I suggested installing threaded rods instead, that could be used to bolt down a wood plate along the lintel. Then the rafters could be nailed to them very easily, producing a stronger joint. He seemed to agree but looked concerned. I knew that look. It meant "this is more expensive and who's going to pay for it?" I allayed the concern by asking him to submit a price for the extra materials.

We spent eight productive hours at the site, but would need at least two to four more to complete the entire slab. Unfortunately, time had run out; it would be dark before they finished; they would have to return in the morning.

It was late afternoon as we prepared to leave for Arusha. Only then did Mathew notice that his jacket missing. Apparently, someone had picked it up and thrown it in the bogged-down truck, thinking it belonged to the driver. Coincidently, we met the truck at an intersection in Karatu a little while later on the way home. The driver, somewhat reluctantly, handed over the jacket.

We wanted to get back quickly, so instead of stopping for a meal, we ate junk food along the way. Deo was sullen for most of the ride back. Fatigued by the new experience of construction work, and worried about the new rattle coming from beneath the mud-caked floorboards, he managed only the occasional mumbled comment, "I need 4-wheel drive… but I have not money…."

I was exhausted too. Deo got us back to Arusha without incident; the car intact, but looking a little battle-weary. He mentioned he would be a little "late for work" in the morning.

CHAPTER 4

A Portrait of Arusha

"To illuminate our real African History,
to clarify our African Present,
to brilliantly project our African Future."

– MAMA KEFA NEPHTHYS

The Arusha Central Market full of amazing foods and people.

Wednesday morning, November 17: I needed a couple of days to rest and reflect.

I had been in Arusha for 10 days now. It felt good that the hardest parts of the projects – foundations and floor slab – were complete, and that the next stage, laying the courses of concrete block walls, was underway. But the pace of events had taken its toll on my energy. I was asking my sixty-four-year-old body to behave like a thirty-year-old's, so I decided a fitness regime would not only keep me in shape but also offset the continual subtle stresses exerted on me by a foreign culture and language.

I opted for a one hour "power walk" first thing in the morning. I also wanted to begin taking care of my diet. The food at the lodge was geared more to pub-style fatty foods, with only token amounts of vegetables. I arranged with Kayanda, the lodge chef, to make up a few "healthy" meals for me from time to time, fish without the batter, steamed veggies, etc., and met with surprisingly little resistance. Within a few days I had started to feel much better.

Life at the Outpost Lodge was comfortable. It was an oasis from the clamorous city life. Guest accommodation was in the form of small rustic cabins scattered among banana trees, palms, flowering trees and various broad-leafed plants. Stone walkways through grassed lawns connected the cabins to open-air rustic dining and lounge areas framed by low brick walls, their pillars supporting wood-framed sheet metal roofing, tickled by low branches of the surrounding *ficus* trees.

I enjoyed the friendly staff who shared their stories with me, many of them similar; a strong desire to better themselves by hard, part-time work at the lodge to support their ongoing education. Theodora Castory, an attractive server in her early twenties, is saving to continue high school at Form Three (our Grade 10) level. It costs 800,000 shillings (Cdn$550) per year. She can't afford to go home, a 12-hour bus ride away, to Iringa, to visit her mother. It's been two years since she's seen her. Goodluck Mashauri, a male server and barman, is completing his part-time studies in hotel management and is bound for success (his mother chose the right name). Daniel Janis, another waiter and former safari guide, has just set up a safari tour business with his silent-partner uncle and is awaiting responses from his website.

During many long conversations with Goodluck, I gathered that the story was common to a lot of young Tanzanians who have left home; education is a continuous stop-start process of working to save enough money to afford the fees for another term of school. But these three were lucky; they had made it through primary school when they were children living at home because, unlike the majority of children in Tanzania, they had parents who managed to scrape together enough money to pay the school fees.

The Outpost Lodge was a haven for Kilimanjaro climbers, safari seekers, backpackers, volunteer workers and NGO workers from all parts of the world. I met very interesting people; French, Germans, Dutch, Israelis, Swedes, as well as some locals who frequent the outdoor lounge and garden area as a peaceful retreat from their crowded neighbourhoods. One such local was a young

English lawyer who came from time to time with her computer for tea and typing. She was working with her lawyer husband at the international tribunal office established here in Arusha for the 1994 Rwanda Crisis, and was very surprised when I mentioned that General Romeo D'Alllaire (commander of the United Nations Assistance Mission for Rwanda during the crisis) was my military college classmate. Yes, it's a small world, and the Outpost certainly contributes to that sense. Perhaps it could be the ideal location to base future projects from.

The cost to stay at the Outpost was probably the best bargain in town. But there were a few quirky things that offset the low cost. The plumbing was bad; hot water for showering slowed to a dribble at times, toilets flushed poorly. (A Roto-Rooter business would make a fortune here. I suggested it to Goodluck and his eyes lit up; "Where can I get trained?") The electrical circuitry is peculiar; I pulled out a plug on an extension cord sticking out of the wall from the outlet below the desk in my room; it shut off the TV in the lounge area. When I plugged in my nifty little Shopper's Drug Mart step-down transformer to charge the battery on my screwgun, the transformer blew up in a puff of smoke. I also discovered that the open wiring coming from a hole in the wall and running around the perimeter of my room to another outlet was supplying power to all the computers in the offices next to my room. It was time to meet the resident "electrician".

"Omari, there is a problem with the outlet in my room. I think the circuit is overloaded, and I'm a little reluctant to plug anything in to it."

"Hakuna Matata, I will install special new outlet next to it."

Images of popping light bulbs, sizzling computers, and smoking wiring circuits flashed through my mind....

"Uhhh… right. No, thanks."

I was convinced these "ingenious" solutions of Omari were definitely overloading the circuitry. I was careful from then on. My computer charger worked (thanks, Mac), but only for 10 minutes at a time before it got overheated.

:ン:

My morning walk had become a pleasurable and interesting event. The Outpost is in an area on the south side of Old Moshi Road in reasonably pleasant surroundings; mostly well-landscaped large private properties. I would circle around the blocks a few times to get an hour's worth of exercise. But the unpaved roads were pot-holed and dusty. Even at 7:00AM in the morning, traffic was busy with commuters trying to a short-cut to the city centre. I would have to change my route.

I discovered the north side of Old Moshi Road was similar; large properties mixed with what I later was told were the finer res-taurants – The Flaming Tree and Pepe's. The big difference? The roads were nicely paved and traffic was minimal. The walk was also a botanical treat. Large pine, *ficus* and jacaranda trees provided shade from the sun. Rows of purple, white and red bougainvillea shrubs adorned the high brick walls protecting private properties. Friendly security guards at well-designed entrance gates greeted me in English. By each walk's end I had passed hundreds of pedestrians and cyclists; mostly well-dressed office workers and domestics, quick to offer a generous smile.

A common sight were young men "taxiing" young female office workers on their bicycles. The women, sitting side-saddle on the cushioned rear wheel carrier seemed quietly comfortable as their cavalier struggled with every peddle stroke. On one walk, I was humoured by the reverse situation; a young woman slowly peddled by with a young man on her carrier. He grinned broadly as he passed, giving me the thumbs-up.

At the half way point of the route is the Arusha High Court, set back a distance from the road, and looking more like a large private colonial residence than a government building. Dozens of men and women were constantly milling about in the outdoor grounds, probably awaiting their turn, or news of a judge's decision involving the plight of family or friends.

Each day I would return to the Outpost, invigorated and in a cheery frame of mind.

⟩⟩✦⟨

On one of my morning walks I saw a sign, "Little Stars Nursery," a short distance from the Outpost. It had an arrow pointing down the road, so I ventured forward and managed to find it, with the help of a local young boy, tucked away at the end of a side road.

The gate was open, so I strolled inside, and was greeted by a friendly middle-aged woman – Helen Osambi, dignified, attractive and colourfully dressed, who introduced herself as the headmistress of the four-classroom nursery. After explaining my projects, she was only too willing to show me around.

In addition to the nursery building, there were also four primary level classrooms arranged in a square with an interior courtyard. I was impressed with the design and construction quality. Lots of windows, high ceilings, a breezeway, separate washrooms for staff and pupils, grassed areas and colourful planting and shrubs. It seemed like the ideal design model. It was a private school financed by two retired African professional women, a former banker and a UN administrator, who obviously placed importance on design aesthetics.

After the tour, Helen insisted I meet Mr. Peniel Nahumu Mero, the school headmaster. I entered his office to see a slightly stooped, weatherworn man nearing retirement. After introductions, Helen whispered a few brief Swahili words to him, and then left. His solemn demeanor surprised me. He asked me to sit down in front of his desk where he proceeded, still without cracking a smile or speaking a word, to write out almost a full page of his resume. I sat there silently, wondering, *Is this guy looking for a job?*

He handed the resume to me and said, in wonderfully African-accented English, "I can help you."

I couldn't believe what a stroke of luck this was. He was a primary school teacher who also worked as a district adult education officer, district education officer and zone inspector of schools. He had been headmaster of four English medium schools: St. Ann's School, Moshi for 4 years; Swift English Medium School for 8 months; Scottish School, Moshi for 3 years; and now at Little Stars. This is exactly what I had been fretting about for two months; how do I find the right people to assess and prioritize the need for new schools?

He continued, "I will help you find the right people to assess and prioritize the need for new schools."

He would be retiring in two weeks and would be available to take me around the various local Ministry of Education offices and meet the necessary contacts.

"Thank you, thank you," I gratefully uttered. "I will contact you then."

He was a busy man. Several visitors were waiting to see him, so, after a really firm handshake, I took my leave.

On the way to the gate, Helen called after me, "Would you like to see a nursery class in progress?"

"Sure."

I don't think I can remember ever witnessing one in progress. This was a treat! She showed me a Level 3 class with 15 or so kids. Classes range from Level 1 for two-year-olds to Level 4 for five-year-olds (for Primary Schools, it's Standard 1 for six-year-olds to Standard 7 for 12-year-olds, and for High School, it's Form 1 for 13-year-olds to Form 6 for 18-year-olds). Helen had the polite little four-year-olds show me the writing in their exercise books.

Supply funds are extremely lacking for even the basics, pencils and paper. They used up every square inch of paper in their books.

After a few more moments of enjoying the teacher and pupils interact, Helen and I left. She walked me to the gate, chatting about the drying up of funds from the donors. Later that day I returned with an armload of exercise books, pencils and coloured pencils. I was surprised how inexpensive the cost was here, about half of that in Canada.

⦂⦂

On another morning's walk, I met Dr. Spear Mwakila, who was going my way. A diminutive, smartly-dressed young man with an incredibly big smile, he looked all of 17-years-old. I mistook him for a high school student on his way to high school. He was actually in his 30's. He had a small herbal medicine clinic that he operated from his home, treating patients with his own natural remedies. He was very interested in my work and strongly suggested I should meet one of his good friends, a farmer, teacher and philanthropist. I agreed, and invited him to breakfast where his own interesting story unfolded.

Spear was the only son in a farming family in a small village in southern Tanzania. He had four sisters. His father had died when he was only five. His mother, according to traditional laws, was then forced to forfeit ownership of all property to the grandparents. Destitute and penniless, they had no choice but to move in with them. Spear's grandfather put him to work tending 100 cattle (at five years old!). When he turned six, his older sister, noticing his aptitude for learning, asked their grandfather to send him to school. He flatly refused.

"The boy must do his duty to the family and work on this farm."

Undaunted, she contacted a sympathetic local teacher who confronted the grandfather: "The law in this country requires all children go to school. If you don't send him to school, we will report you, and you will be fined."

The grandfather later summoned Spear: "If you go to school, you are no longer my grandson."

He began his new life, living with the family of the teacher, who was more than willing to sponsor this young prodigy. Spear excelled through all levels of primary and secondary school, and worked his way through college by traveling through various towns and cities selling T-shirts to tourists.

By the age of 26, he had a degree in herbal medicine from the Tanzania Institute of Agriculture where he had learned about the chemical properties of native trees and plants. Through years of continued research in towns and villages, in various botanically "ripe" regions around the country, he developed herbal concoctions that have successfully treated patients suffering from HIV, tuberculosis, high blood pressure, diabetes and malaria. Although his reputation is growing, his practice at the moment is limited to working from his home office.

Armed with his successes, he recently attended an international medical conference in Dar Es Salaam, where he hoped a western sponsor would help fund his dream for a new clinic in Arusha and help him to purchase land where he would grow his specialty herbs, plants and trees. Many were impressed by his presentation, but when asked to divulge his herbal formulae, he declined, so any interest quickly evaporated. One could understand; what would be in it for them?

Spear showed me photos of his family. His three daughters seemed to be a chip off the old block. Their school marks were in the upper 90s. He also showed me a photo of a group of young orphans that he works with in his spare time. I was impressed with his energy and enthusiasm, and hoped we would keep in touch. After finishing our breakfast we parted and agreed that sometime tomorrow we could get together again, this time, with his friend.

Only a few hours later, he called me.

"Mister Roy, I have Andrew Titus with me. He would like to meet you today."

"Uhhh… well… OK, I guess." I could have been uncomfortable since I had been planning to catch up on paperwork, but in truth, I was delighted and curious to meet him. "Can you bring him to the Outpost, say, at 4:00PM today?"

It was 1:30PM.

"Can we meet right away?" Spear asked.

At 1:35PM (they must have already been in the lobby), I was being introduced to a tall imposing "gentle giant" of a man, sixty-ish, soft spoken, dressed in khaki and sporting a wide leather safari hat (that he never removed). A few minutes later, the three of us were sipping tea and eating banana bread in the Outpost outdoor lounge. Andrew was anxious to meet me to discuss his education project.

In the village of Kikatiti, not far from Arusha, he owned a five-acre farm, where he grew maize and kidney beans. Retired from formal teaching at primary schools, secondary schools and at a teachers college, he was now passionate about teaching vocational skills, carpentry, welding and sewing, to disadvantaged children and teens in his community. Classes were held in whatever small building space was available on his property. His dream was to build a primary school and vocational school on a vacant section

Alan, Andrew Titus, and Dr. Spear enjoy tea and banana bread while discussing future projects.

of his property, but he needed help with funding. I said I might be interested in it as a future project of our organization, that we were still in a period of gestation, and that it would be some time before serious discussions could happen. It would come down to our future fund-raising successes back in Canada. He was more than happy enough with that and before we parted, I agreed to take him up on his invitation for a visit to his farm before I left Tanzania.

✣

Arusha is a city of experiences that are both fascinating and frustrating.

My business routine included regular trips from the Outpost Lodge to the city centre where I frequented the NBC bank, Kase's bookstore and the photocopy shop, all within a short walking distance of each other. The trip was along the main east artery, Old Moshi Road, which ends at a traffic circle at the city centre. In the centre of the traffic circle is the Clock Tower, a reference point for tourist directions. From there, looking to the north, one could see the spectacular sight of Mount Meru.

From the traffic circle the route continues west through the centre of the city, along Sokoine Road, framed on each side by an endless proliferation of two- and three-storey commercial buildings, nondescript in style, but exuberant in colour, with small narrow-fronted shops at street level. Street vendors with their hand-drawn carts are stationed on corners where pedestrian traffic is plentiful.

The carts are overloaded, some with fruit and vegetables, some with various artistic trinketry, and others with cheap electronics.

One vendor had an amazing stack of stereos, ghetto blasters and speakers, all precariously piled on top of each other at least five feet high on his cart. I was amused at the thought of a customer selecting, and then trying to remove, the one at the bottom.

Vendors who didn't have carts had managed to bargain with shop owners to hang their portable wares – crafts, artwork, maps, translation pamphlets – on any available space on the shop walls and adjacent screens, providing wonderfully complex and colourful displays. I felt a sense of admiration for their time-consuming daily regimen of setting up and dismantling their merchandise, but also a certain sadness for what I imagined was little financial return.

The city's Central Market, a few blocks north of Sokoine Road, is the hub of pedestrian hustle and bustle on weekdays as well as weekends. At the centre is the original open-air structure, a flimsy ferrous fabrication of post and beam frames covered with corrugated metal sheeting. Inside it, rows of stalls sell everything from nuts to notions, all meticulously arranged. That, together with the array of different fabrics worn by the crowds of female shoppers, presents a visual cornucopia of colourful patterns and textures.

The fast pace of the city's growth in the last decade has resulted in the area of the Central Market spilling over into the surrounding streets where vendors neatly lay out their wares, mostly fabrics, fruits and vegetables, on blankets, or whatever sidewalk or ground space is available. Many of the narrow-fronted stores there are "one-item" shops; one sells the full spectrum of colourful Maasai blankets, another an array of fabrics, another countless seeds and nuts, and yet another, jars of delicious looking spices. The shop design is very basic; typically, about eight feet wide, with a roll-up metal-slatted screen exposing just enough area for the customer to stand in front of a counter which extends across the full width of the room. In the shallow space behind the counter, on the back wall, the wares are neatly displayed on floor-to-ceiling shelving within easy reach of the proprietor.

I marveled at the many custom-order tailors, male and female, that set up sewing machines on sidewalks in front of their shops.

Arusha street vendors sewing suits and garments for sale.

As an advertisement of their talent, they would craft away, displaying a selection of fabrics along with completed orders on the shop's front walls.

I was drawn in to one shop that displayed a fabric that had a pattern of beautiful African browns, blacks and golds, colours that would look perfect on Maureen. I interrupted the sewing of the handsome, well-dressed, middle-aged woman with my idea to order a custom skirt for my wife.

Of course, the obvious question came: "How big is she?"

My typical male response with curving hand gestures didn't seem to help her. She summoned her teenage daughter from inside the shop and stood her in front of me.

"About this size?" she queried.

"Uhh, yes… about that size… I think so."

"No problem," she said, saving the situation. "I will make it one-size-fits-all."

Arusha was not a typical tourist town; there were not a lot of other white faces. They mostly came for the safaris and Mount Kilimanjaro. The main market catered to the local population. Visitors that did venture into the city centre, however, were persistently hassled by hawkers selling maps, translation booklets and, interestingly enough, foreign newspapers.

The oddest feature of the city was the way storm water was handled on most of the streets. On one or both sides of the street was a deep open concrete channel, two feet wide at the bottom and sloping up to four feet wide at the top, that I'm certain carried storm water very effectively, but at great expense to parking and pedestrian traffic. In the centre of the city, the channels are lined with concrete, but farther out of town, they are dirt ditches. Narrow bridges are placed at regular intervals but many, usually the young and more athletic, can be seen leaping, often with casual ballet-like elegance, across the gap.

A big concern to locals is traffic congestion along the main east-west artery. Old Moshi Road and Sokoine Road are the only direct route through the city. The traffic is painfully slow, pollution levels, off the charts. Government street planning, according to Jacob's acute political criticisms, is either non-existent or unable to keep pace with the haphazard growth of commercial and office buildings that seem to arbitrarily crop up in both the city's centre as well as the surrounding districts.

To avoid Sokoine congestion, Deo preferred to maneuver his taxi through the side streets, where even there, the experience was equally painful. Most roads are unmaintained, uneven, full of potholes, and with large protruding rocks that threaten to disembowel a car's underbelly. Small restaurants and "corner stores" are crowded together with houses that vary from modest to substandard. Some even have a few goats and cows crammed into their small yard.

On one occasion, Deo and I bumped wildly from pothole to pothole through a side street, splashing mud on the occasional unwary pedestrian. Then we came to a standstill. Short-cutting cars from both directions had also been stopped. We waited five or fen minutes, before I impatiently asked, "What's going on, Deo?"

"I don't know. This is not normal. Maybe we should have a look."

We walked ahead to an opening in the traffic where several men were blocking the road. Pulling strenuously on a tether rope, they were not having any success rescuing a cow that had slid down into the muddy storm channel. She sat there in the mud, on her buckled legs, seemingly content just to be out of the traffic. The men kept pulling until finally, the bedraggled beast gave in and clawed her way up and out. The cars slowly dispersed. We ended up following the cow for a while, the owner struggling hard to keep her moving, and finally managed to pass her as she loudly bellowed her displeasure.

I ran the gauntlet along Sokoine Road every time I visited Majengo. As described earlier, it was the slum area of the city, located at the western end of Sokoine Road, two or three miles from the city centre. The quality of the street life and building construction deteriorated gradually as you headed west. In Majengo, open-air buildings, shantily constructed from whatever materials were cheaply available, housed various trade businesses, furniture makers, welders, joinery and window fabricators, alongside bars and food stores. Hand-pulled wooden carts, loaded to deliver food, furniture, construction materials, competed with vehicles for road space. They were almost as numerous as vehicles and factored heavily in slowing traffic to a standstill at times.

Food vendors from the farming areas unloaded their pickup trucks and set up their vegetables in unevenly-trodden grassy areas of land alongside Sokoine Road, usually in front of public buildings that had available open space, and as far into the city as they could get. Farmer vendors who didn't have vehicles laboriously pulled their overloaded wooden carts, two or three persons abreast, many miles to these locations where they squatted on the ground alongside blankets that displayed a variety of produce, including carrots, bananas, pineapple and bags of rice, all neatly laid out in rows. Business was brisk as the food was sold at bargain prices to business employees stocking up on groceries during a lunch hour that spanned from 12:00 to 2:00PM.

Vehicles jostled with hordes of jaywalking pedestrians. Considering the narrow margin of error between passing vehicles and pedestrians, I was amazed when told of the relatively few accidents. And it was quite worthy to note that, unlike in the west, road rage in Arusha seemed to be non-existent. The Tanzanian temperament was one of extraordinary patience; horn-honking was at a minimum, and drivers respectfully maneuvered around each other, signaling thanks with a little hand wave.

But the pollution levels remained difficult to cope with, especially because of the constant traffic congestion. The smog was so bad at times, one could barely breathe. No exhaust emission controls existed on the majority of old vehicles. I remembered reading somewhere that respiratory disease led the causes of death in Tanzania. After one return trip to the Majengo site, I usually needed the next day to recover. During one trip in someone else's taxi (Deo had not been available) where the windows were permanently stuck in the down position (at least that was what the taxi driver had insisted was the case), the acrid billowing exhaust fumes were so bad, I had put my hat over my face to minimize the intake. Not much help. Then I'd had an idea that seemed to work well. I took off one of my sweaty wool socks, folded it in half and covered my mouth with it. I placed it over my face to inhale, long and slow. I took it off to exhale. Hey: I was desperate! Needless to say, I would be "stocking" up on proper facemasks soon.

✳✳✳

During my morning stroll on Friday, November 19, I was feeling a little more comfortable among the crowds of pedestrians commuting to work, not caring if I stood out as I cheerily greeted every passerby. I was in a great mood; the school projects were progressing without any serious problems. Was it always going to be this smooth, I wondered?

Normally, I would have been a little cautious passing young, opportunistically-minded men hanging around the streets waiting for a white tourist to "walk and talk with." On one occasion I caught the eye of a young man as I passed and greeted him with a "jambo." A little later, I could hear the quick pace of footsteps approaching from behind. The same young man had caught up to me. He introduced himself as James Kaaya and, smiling, asked if I needed any help with directions, or general tourist information.

I would normally have shooed away his unwanted solicitation, but on that occasion, I remembered that my wife Maureen had wanted me to pick up some art: as gifts for the kids (at 27, 29 and 31 years old, we still call them that), as well as for some for our friends. After chatting for a bit I asked if he could recommend a good place to buy fabric wall hangings. He told me that there were many small shops with local artwork scattered around the city, some hidden away in back streets. He took me to one, a large ramshackle warehouse down a side street that, surprisingly, was only a short distance from the lodge.

The "Africa-Op" was an artist co-op enterprise that took advantage of cheap available warehouse space to sell their work at bargain prices. The building was a wood-framed structure, its roof and walls covered in corrugated metal sheeting, and filled with rows of shelves that, to my delight, contained hundreds of fabric art pieces to choose from. I was surprised that only one young staff person manned the store. I was like a kid in a candy shop as he helped me rummage through scores of shelved items, then unfolded them and lay them on the floor so that I could see their patterns. Large heavy cotton sheets, hand painted with images of giraffes, elephants and zebras, framed in bold colourful graphic patterns, were exactly what I had envisaged: local crafting, not overly commercialized, and easy to pack in my carry-on.

Because business was at a standstill that day, the young salesman was eager to accommodate me despite my indecision. And he didn't mind that we were leaving the place in a mess with fabrics strewn over most of the floor area. James was also keen to help, offering his recommendations for what he considered to be the best picks. He also suggested that it would not be inappropriate to haggle over the price, so I did (with some success) and then we left the place, both feeling pretty satisfied with our artistic adventure.

I was lucky to have met James; I would never have found these hidden treasures without him. How could I not reward him for his enterprising efforts? Before parting, I offered him a healthy "fee." He rewarded me with two of the most common and wonderful characteristics I have come to discover of Tanzanians; a broad-grinned smile and a hearty handshake.

In the afternoon it was Majengo site visit number three. I was happy to see the floor slab completed and the concrete block walls rising. I took a few measurements of the new washroom layout as a check, and noticed the washroom width was too small by 8 inches. Since only three courses of blocks had been laid at this point, Hemedi said it would be no problem to move the walls over.

Later in the afternoon, Teddy arrived from her nursery school to have lunch. After the usual warm greeting, she continued with her efforts to speak English and asked, in the halting English I had become accustomed to, "Babu, you would like to come to our church this Sunday?"

"That would be fine," I said. "Thank you. What should I expect?"

"There will be lots of entertainment. You will enjoy."

"Ahsante, I will be there."

⁓

Today we had planned to select the doors and windows at local fabrication shops. Hemedi took Jacob and me to a door joinery shop in a semi-industrial area on hectic Sokoine Road. It was an airy ramshackle shed with sheet metal walls and roof. The floor was covered with wood shavings and sawdust and looked very much like a fire hazard, but business was good and they had many styles of doors in different wood types to choose from. I opted for the paneled doors made from a reddish-coloured Jacaranda wood, similar to our Western Red Cedar.

The next stop was an interesting study in extremely limited space planning. The window "shop," close to the joinery, was operated by a welder who somehow managed to squeeze his equipment and materials, probably without a permit, in a long, 4-foot wide, alleyway between two other businesses that probably rented the space as an opportunity for some additional income. We maneuvered ourselves along the selection of different window types and after finding the style we wanted, we placed our order.

Before leaving them, I asked about the schedule. Jacob and Hemedi advised that we could be finished as early as December 9th. Just over a month to build a school – incredible!

∗✗∗

At church on Sunday morning, I was not disappointed. After an hour of listening to the expected bible readings and minister's sermon, the "entertainment" began. A couple of guitarists, the keyboarder and the drummer took their places. For an hour, separate groups of parishioners took turns coming up to the front of the pews to sing and dance. They had such incredible voices and well-synchronized natural rhythm that those still in the pews couldn't help but clap to the beat or sing along. Some got up to dance wherever they could find space in the aisles. It was a wonderful free-for-all. These folks sure knew how to "celebrate" mass.

After church, I went to visit Jacob's family again. Their daughters Anna, Muchu and Febu had been asking about me since my first visit back in September. Anna and Muchu were anxious to see me. I sat for an hour or so in their tiny living room, listening to Jacob's translation of their excited stories about what they were learning at school, including English lessons. They were only pre-schoolers, but they proudly rhymed off all the numbers from one to 50 in English. What a treat to hear their wonderful accents.

CHAPTER 5

WALLS RISING

"Sticks in a bundle are unbreakable."

– *KENYAN PROVERB*

Solid and handcrafted school walls rising at the Gongali site.

Monday, November 22, was a day of sorting out construction costs with Mathew. We met at the Outpost and spent a few hours going over the first three progress claims. During the site visits, I had discovered that Fabian's contract price was based on his assumptions about how to build, and not necessarily on what was drawn and specified on my plans. Simply put, he was building it his own (traditional) way. It was understandable that he would have had little experience reading aspects of technical drawings: building sections, details, symbols for light fixtures, etc. So, through Mathew's interpretations, we agreed on a few compromises, which, in practical terms, meant adding more material to make the building a little stronger, for example, spacing the roof rafters closer together, or adding missed items such as light fixtures and switches.

Then an unfortunate incident occurred: there was a significant discrepancy in the last claim. It was unusually high. Reviewing the contract, we discovered a large typing error in his list of materials. During the tender when I insisted on a typed list, Philemon had had to search out a typist in Karatu (no one owned or had a use for one in the village) but the document was not carefully checked, and I hadn't noticed it either. The 2,400 concrete blocks @ 1,500 Tanzanian shillings (TSh) per block totaled 360,000 TSh instead of the correct 3,600,000 TSh. Leaving off a zero would add 3,240,000 shillings to the project, and put me over my contingency limit. We would have to meet with Philemon and Fabian to decide how to cut costs to make up for it. Mathew, in his usual reassuring way, said, "No. Philemon will have to sell some cattle, maybe six or seven, to pay for it. It is the village responsibility."

"Mathew, I can't do that. It was an honest mistake and besides, I don't want to put any additional hardship on the village. It could create some resentment with the villagers. We'll figure something out."

This revelation made it mandatory for us to keep track of increasing costs. I didn't want to run out of funds and go home with the schools unfinished. We agreed that the solution was for the builders to submit claims for progress payments that listed materials and labour costs checked off against the contract list. Also, they were to provide a separate list of the additional costs, so that I could amend the contract amount accordingly and keep track of my dwindling contingency money.

Mathew admitted his bookkeeping was a little casual (he had all his paperwork stuffed in a large envelope), so right after our meeting, I suggested a visit to Kase's bookstore. As with Jacob, he was very appreciative when I bought him the basic office supplies to help keep his papers in order. This time, however, I added a calculator for both of them.

As we parted, I sensed a certain malaise in his demeanor: "Mathew, you look a little distracted."

"Yes, I was thinking about when I would be able to visit the site with you again. There are so many things all happening in my life now."

"I'll be OK going there on my own," I assured him.

"But now we have to correct this concrete block error; I need to be there."

"You're probably right… so what else is going on?"

"My wife Rose is expecting a baby and I'm thinking of leaving my job at the hotel for a better offer."

"Really? When?"

"As soon as we set up an appointment."

"No, I meant the baby…."

"Any day now."

Our next scheduled visit to the site was in two days.

"Well, then, it's definite, you must stay," I continued. "A new job, eh? Where?"

"Yes, at a much better hotel. The owners are more supportive of their staff. I will leave on December 2 after my last big effort at the hotel, a large convention. My restaurant staff will have a big challenge so I agreed to stay."

On Tuesday, November 23, Jacob met me at the Outpost, armed with the next claim for payment, to make another visit to the bank. I also planned to withdraw an amount for Philemon that Mathew and I had agreed on. The bank visit was usually a pleasant experience. Maternus, the bank manager, or in his absence one of his assistants, Godwin or Shabami, would greet us with a smile and a hearty Tanzanian handshake and we would chat a bit before he left to get our cash.

That day was an exception; no one was in the offices. We had to get in line downstairs with the dozens or so patiently queued up in front of a few overworked tellers. It could take over an hour.

We went downstairs and noticed that one teller whose only job it was to issue ATM cards had only a few customers, so we approached him and tried to short-circuit our efforts. His disinterest miffed Jacob, who pleaded with him for some time before the teller's resistance fizzled and he directed us to an unmarked door at the end of the tellers' windows.

Holding Jacob back, he unlocked it, held it open for me and ushered me in. It was an experience to remember. The room was no bigger than a janitor's closet (it probably had been), measuring about four feet wide and eight feet long with a counter and a glass partition (probably bullet-proof) separating me from a stone-faced middle-aged man who, without a word or nod of greeting, pointed to a slot in the glass. I offered a smile (that was rejected) and slid the withdrawal slip through.

Crammed between this fellow and the exit door behind him were large stacks of bundled cash, amounting to at least several hundred million shillings, piled up on shelves on one wall, and, on the opposite wall, a small counter and what seemed to be an old-fashioned money counting machine. The room was not properly ventilated; it was so hot and stifling that even the cash was sagging. The teller picked up a droopy bundle of shillings, loaded it on top of the machine, which quickly devoured it, whirring in appreciation, and then the machine spit out neat little bundles of

100,000 shillings at a time. He deftly bundled them all together to form one large bundle, put it in a metal "laundry chute" door in the wall below him, pushed a button, and as dispassionate as ever, gestured for me to open the metal door at my knees, from where the money could be extracted. The purpose of the next breath I took after exiting the tiny room was twofold: relief and oxygen.

The next day, Deo drove us to Gongali for our fourth visit. Mathew had phoned the previous evening and insisted on coming. Rose was close. She was still at home, but a friend of the family was with her, so she would be OK. We met Philemon at the Paradise Restaurant office where he did his usual "cash and dash"; Marco's delivery truck was waiting.

During the five mile drive to the school site, Mathew clarified that the village was actually many farms spread out over a large area. What was considered the village centre was only a handful of buildings, the mayor's office and several small stores that sold only a small amount of packaged foods and miscellaneous household items. Vehicular traffic in the area is minimal; there are only a few roads. A lot of the farms and homes have long trails leading from the main road. The way to Philemon's home, for example, is simply a trail carved out by his motorcycle. Villagers commonly walk many miles to visit each other. I could distinguish their distant faint trails that seemed to arbitrarily zig-zag through the fields.

"So what happens at Christmas? Is there a hall where all can meet and celebrate? How do families celebrate Christmas?" I asked.

"Except for church on Christmas Eve, we do not have large gatherings. For three days we visit our closest neighbors and have a good time drinking and telling stories. On Christmas day, we prepare our favorite meal of goat, chicken or beef, with rice pilau, and enjoy a long feast."

"There are more cars at Christmas," he continued. "Some villagers who have left for good paying jobs in the city return to be with families, but most return by buses that are overcrowded and slow during this time."

I mentioned that it was pretty much the same routine in Canada.

"What about gifts? Back home on Christmas Eve or Christmas morning in Canada, families open presents given to each other. It is a special time, especially for children, who become very excited."

"We mostly do not have that," Mathew replied. "We buy cards for our friends and neighbors to show our appreciation for helping us when we have problems."

The weather was holding out; it hadn't rained since the last visit, so progress at the site was good. A half-mile from the site, I was excited to see the school's walls extending above the horizon: "Mathew, this is great; the school is taking shape and will be able to be seen from many miles away," I said. "Classrooms rising from the clay."

The walls were completed to the lintel level, and the workers were working on the formwork and concrete work for the last few posts and were about to start the formwork for the lintel beams. I got there just in time to explain to Fabian that the rebar spacing in the 12-inch deep centre beam in each classroom had to be a minimum 9 inches instead of the 4 inches he was planning.

I would need Mathew's help translating this to Fabian, but I could see him off in the distance, pacing, with his cell phone glued to his ear. I wondered how Rose was doing. He would end up phoning her every hour or so for the rest of the day.

Fabian's aggressive scheduling of just over four weeks to build the school meant that the major construction of the septic pit

Pouring concrete posts, one bucket at a time, at the Gongali site.

would not be finished until a month or so after the school building was completed if rain was light. But if the heavy rains came, it would have to wait until the dry season next April-May. When he explained the fifty-foot-deep hole that was to be dug, I questioned, "You mean 15 *feet* deep."

"No, *fifty* feet. We don't want to pump it out for fifty years."

The ten-foot-diameter hole was to be 49 feet deep. It sounded a little dangerous to build.

"Will there not be a risk of wall collapse? And what if you encounter groundwater?"

"No, this ground is very hard and we are confident it will be dry at the bottom. Water in this area is at least two hundred feet down."

When they explained they had never dug quite that deep before, I certainly had my doubts, but I wasn't about to dampen their enthusiasm.

Philemon was anxious to start classes as soon as the building was complete. Given that the school registration would not be possible without toilets, and that with rains looming it was too late to start the deep hole, they decided to build temporary toilets a short distance away from the building. When the building's toilets were finished, the extra toilets would not be a duplication; in fact, they thought they would make good "visitor's toilets."

The village was beginning to buzz with excitement about the school project. Since it would be finished in two short weeks, they had started to think about landscaping. Volunteers were digging holes around the perimeter of the school to plant *minyaa* trees to protect from wind and dust. The location of an entrance pathway and parking area was being discussed. They seemed to have it well in hand; I didn't feel a need to become involved.

At midday, the women arrived to cook the usual staple for lunch, ugali and spinach. I enjoyed the bright colours of their dresses and headgear – in such sharp contrast to the worker's drab tees and loose fitting pants. Everywhere in Tanzania, even when men were dressed in their best, the women stood out, with their long skirts emphasizing their graceful walk, their delicate wraps slung over their shoulders, and their heads wrapped carefully in a swirl of fabric; all in a vibrant array of patterns and colours. The exception, of course, was the Maasai men with their equally colourful traditional wraps.

I brought my bag of tools to the site, hoping to contribute some work, but it was premature. During lunch, I demonstrated how strongly wood could be joined using my screw-gun (drill). Not surprisingly, they had never seen one and were excitedly lining up to try it out when alas, the battery failed. Without the charger that had blown up in a puff of smoke a few days earlier, this proved to be the last time my drill would see action in Tanzania.

I knew the roof framing should be well under way by my next visit, and I looked forward to helping out. I love wood framing; it was the best part of building; so much visual return so quickly. I had done a fair amount of building over the years, as a contractor to support my architectural studies and more recently, to design

Local Gongali women preparing "ugali" for the workers' lunch.

and build my own home, but I had made it clear to Fabian that he was the "boss" and I would follow his instructions. However, given my "take-charge" personality, I knew trying to let someone else hold the reins would be a challenging experience.

Later in the afternoon, Philemon announced it was time to leave for a visit to his home to meet his family. I looked quizzically at Mathew, "What? You never mentioned...."

"Yes, Babu Alan, this is a special surprise for you."

The drive from the school to Philemon's house through a maze of trails was an effort for Deo; if it wasn't for Philemon's detailed directions we would have been lost. His home is befitting a village mayor. It sits on one of the hills in Gongali, a few miles from the actual village centre, with a magnificent panoramic view of the countryside below, of small hardy black acacia trees and grey-green shrubs scattered among sparsely planted crops of maize and pigeon pea.

Philemon's wife Anna and their four children greeted Mathew, Deo and me and ushered us into their small, dimly lit living/dining area. After introducing us to them, Anna, with a gentle firmness, and in an unusually low and resonant voice, shooed the kids who had previously eaten, into another room. They would be summoned later for a photo shoot. We proceeded to feast on the family's favorite meal reserved only for special occasions: chicken stew, rice, spinach and pineapple.

We had an entertaining time, joking about the worker's various personalities and humorous antics, and feeling good about the school's progress. I noticed a sign on their wall that conjured up the usual trite "home sweet home", or something similar. I asked Philemon about it. When he told me, I laughed at the translation:

"*Ndao ni ya wawili, Watatu ni ibilisi*"

["Marriage is for two, Three is for the devil"].

It was a statement, I guessed, against the traditional views of polygamy, especially of the Maasai men who still married many wives.

Then I raised the subject of the "official opening."

"Can you describe what is planned?"

"There will be much activity," Philemon replied. "We have been discussing traditional celebrations with music, dance, speeches and much food. Perhaps there will be roast goat."

"And will they be wearing traditional dress?"

"Those who have it will wear it."

After we had eaten, Anna summoned the reluctant children for the family photo shoot around the table. Then Philemon led Mathew, Deo and I outside to enjoy the view of a magnificent sunset. Philemon and I chatted while Mathew decided to phone his wife Rose for an update on her condition.

"Everyone in the village is very excited about the school," Philemon said. "They are planting the *minyaa* trees around the perimeter of the schoolyard, and we have also decided to have some flower areas."

Philemon pointed out his prize cactus plant. "As a special feature," he said, "I will donate my rare cactus that we will locate near the entrance to the school."

I thought about the site "master plan" that I had envisaged, which would lay out all the design elements: future phase classrooms, office building, teacher's residence, pathways, windbreaks, parking areas, and perhaps a garden. I was upset with myself for not having provided at least a rough sketch for Philemon to use as a guide to locate the windbreak. But it seemed they were making their own decisions, and ones that were probably well thought through. I would just have to let go and trust again that local knowledge and experience would reign successfully.

"Are you leaving room for the future buildings?" I offered.

"We will only plant trees at the east side where the winds are," he said. "Can you do a sketch for us for the buildings?"

"Certainly," I replied in relief.

Mathew came over. He had just finished a 20-minute call to Rose, and looked a little perplexed:

"Well, how is she?" I asked.

"She's very tired, but she's OK. Nothing's happening yet. We were talking about a name for the baby."

"Are you hoping for a boy or a girl?"

"A brother for Lissa would be nice, but we will be happy either way. We have decided that if it is a boy, we will name it after you, Babu Alan, and if it is a girl, after your wife Maureen."

"Wow! Whooh! Thank you. And Maureen will... we both thank you. But why...?"

Mathew explained that it is a custom for many Tanzanians to name their child after a person who had made a significant contribution to their lives at the time. In the case of his daughter Lissa, she was named after Rose's friend who rushed her to the hospital when Lissa was born.

I felt extremely honored, and returned the compliment: "If it wasn't for you and the village of Gongali, we would still be looking for their first village primary school project."

I will always remember Thursday, November 25, as the "Day of the Children."

Teddy and Jacob had planned for me to visit Teddy's nursery school while classes were still in progress, before the one-month shutdown from the end of November until the first week in January. Apart from the "Little Stars" experience, this would be my first time to really see a class in action. I assumed it would be a time of pleasant enjoyment and quiet observation.

Well! Nothing of the sort!

When Deo dropped me off, Teddy greeted me with a big hug, and took me to the first of four classrooms, where the predominant age of the children in each classroom ranged from two to six. I

One of Teddy's classes at her existing Majengo Nursery School.

was introduced to the teacher, who then raised her arms, and after the pause typical of a great maestro, gestured the beginning of their pre-rehearsed song of tribute to Babu Alan. I was in a state of disbelief. The little kids were standing and singing, with a bit of choreography thrown in, a few English lines that Teddy had composed, repeating the phrase over and over about a dozen times:

"How are you, this morning?
We are happy little children."

It was at once, a moving and humorous experience. They were singing with such energy and determination. Some had trouble remembering the words, and were trying to take cues from the proudly animated ones next to them. A few wide-eyed little ones were silently looking around, appearing a little confused and overwhelmed. At the "good morning" part, pairs were shaking each other's hand, their motions delightfully exaggerated. But it was their wonderful African accents that were so memorable. I was glad I had remembered to bring my camera to videotape some of this performance to share the experience with family and friends back home.

The experience was repeated in all four classrooms, with different phrases and choreography, to my equal enjoyment and amazement. Teddy's English for the wording was limited, but despite her awkward phrasing, it was no less meaningful, or beautiful:

"Shake, shake Mango tree.
Mango green, mango yellow
One for you and one for me."

"Welcome welcome.

Thank you Babu, for education.

We're not fear anybody, because of education."

But it was Class Four that I'm sure Teddy reserved for last; on purpose:

"Babu Alan, Babu Alan, (clap, clap, clap)

Babu Alan, how we wonder you are.

We love you so much, Babu Alan, (clap, clap, clap)

Babu Alan, how we wonder you are."

When it was over, I was red-eyed and still a little overwhelmed, so I was thankful to retire to Teddy's office to recover. I hugged her, saying, "Thank you so much for this incredible gift. I will never forget it."

"Babu Alan, I also have another gift."

She had crafted a very detailed drawing of an ostrich using feathers (probably from local chickens) mounted on a large piece of cardboard.

"You are a good craftsperson. This is very well done."

"Crafting is my hobby," she said. "It helps to relax me. When you look at this back in Canada, remember we will always be thinking of Babu Alan."

⋗⋗⋖⋖

The next couple of days were spent catching up on writing, responding to e-mails, and sorting out the project cost overruns. I needed extra funds for the projects, so I was glad that I had prearranged with my bank to give my bookkeeper, Esther, authorization to access my account and wire me an additional few thousand dollars. Within a couple of days of my request, she e-mailed back with her usual wry humour: "...enjoying my new life here in the Bahamas... just kidding, I watched them push the send button."

Mathew phoned on Friday to advise on Rose's situation. Things were getting close.

"We took her to hospital this morning. She was in distress," Mathew said.

"I hope she's OK," I said.

"Nothing to worry about. The doctor said everything is normal. He is confident that it will be an easy delivery, not like Lissa. Her delivery was very long and difficult, and painful for Rose.

"I will remain here now," he continued. "And I will keep you informed."

"Mathew, that's not necessary."

"Yes, I want to share this with you."

"OK," I said. (And felt flattered he thought I was important enough.)

At breakfast the next day, an excited Mathew phoned.

A healthy little Maureen had been born at 5:30AM on Saturday, 27 November, 2010.

Proud father Mathew, with Lissa and little Maureen.

CHAPTER 6

BRICKS, WOOD, SHEET METAL

"All I know is that every time I go to Africa, I am shaken to my core."

– STEPHEN LEWIS

Builder Hemedi at the Majengo site that now has a ridge beam.

On Monday, November 29, Jacob came to the Outpost to discuss the roof framing. The timber had to be purchased soon. Hemedi was willing to follow the plans, but since some of the large timber sizes I specified were not available, Hemedi asked Jacob to convince me that it would be OK to use smaller ones. I decided to go along with it, to trust his experience.

My plan for the afternoon was for Deo to drive me to the bank and then to do some shopping for a generator, a drill, and perhaps a circular saw to help with the roof framing at both projects. I thought the equipment would be a good investment for future school projects. Jacob offered to accompany me on my errands on his way back to the Majengo site.

The banking was routine. We were lucky to bump into the manager's assistant, Shabami Mbegu, when we entered. He announced he was the father of a new baby girl, his first child. He grinned when I told him how the timing coincided with Mathew's baby, and then left to get our cash.

While waiting, I took the opportunity to discuss the logistics of the official school opening. Jacob explained that it would be a community celebration, with at least 50 children; that it would be nice to have food and drinks for everyone, and could I help out? Then there was the presentation of a gift to Teddy's new school from my bookkeeper, Esther. Esther had forwarded a personal donation to be equally used for supplies for the two schools.

"What does Teddy think about the food?" I asked. "Can she prepare a list?"

"Already done; meat, rice pilau, and soft drinks and ice cream for the kids."

I hesitated to ask. "What about the cost?"

"I priced it out already, approximately two hundred thousand shillings... but if that's too much, we can lower—"

"—No, that will be OK."

Next was Esther's gift.

"What we can do," I suggested, "is package up the supplies in a cardboard box with Esther's name on it, saying, 'From your Canadian friend, Esther,' and you take a photo while I present it to Teddy. The photo would be a nice momento for Esther."

Jacob had an alternative suggestion: "Uniforms are much more urgently needed than pencils and paper. The community has agreed to donate supplies and furniture."

"Good idea. But there may not be time to organize it."

"Hakuna matata, Alan. My wife Birgita is an excellent tailor."

I have to give him credit; he was quick on the draw on that one.

When Mbegu returned with the bundles, I handed Jacob 370,000 shillings that would take care of the food, the gift, and some additional money for his administration costs.

The rest of the afternoon was a frenzy of rushing around from shop to shop looking for tools. We only had two hours. I was getting a little anxious, but confident of success; after all... every year in Canada, I go through a similar experience several hours before the shops close on Christmas Eve.

Deo knew the shops well. He drove us close to the Arusha Central Market, where, in a one-block area, small shops selling small portions of construction goods huddled against each other in fierce competition. Due to lack of space, one shop sold nothing but sheet goods – ceiling boards, plywood and drywall – while another sold only plumbing fittings. Goods spilled out into the streets, piled up on roughly-built concrete landings in front of the open-faced shops. Young shopkeepers, sitting back against the shop-front walls on tilted chairs, watched indifferently as endless streams of passing motorcycles, bicycles and diesel-fume-spewing cars and trucks deposited reddish-brown clouds of dirt and road dust on their merchandise.

The sequence of subsequent events is worth itemizing. We "Arusha"-ed around. After a few shop visits, our first major disappointment: circular electric saws were unheard of. I resigned myself to settling for just the drill. At the next shop, we bought their only drill. But they didn't have the Robertson bit I needed for the boxes of screws I had brought to Tanzania, nor the drill bits I needed. But the Tanga General Shop had them. At Tanga, there was no Robertson bit, but we got the wood drill bits. They didn't have an extension cord, and referred us to Wakil Electrics across the street. The server there gave us a choice: a custom fabrication of wire and plugs to any length, or a more expensive wind-up one. We couldn't wait the half hour it would take for the custom work, so we settled on the wind-up. Next was the generator. They were popular. Every second shop was selling them, but there were so many to choose from. They stocked stacks of inexpensive ones made in Korea, India and China, but I remembered the previous advice of Charles at the Outpost: "Go with a Japanese model." A young shopkeeper had one at the right price. But I had to have him shut off the loud blaring rap music that was competing with his product description. On closer inspection, we noticed the generator was used, not new. Most of them were used, so we gave up on these small shops in favor of Benson's, the larger, bustling, modern shop run by some very successful East Indian merchants, who recommended an appropriate brand new three-horsepower, four-stroke Japanese model. Loud fuming two-strokes were out of the question. I insisted on a demo. The salesman took the machine outside onto the busy main street to give it a test. It was hard to start. When it finally did start, it ran erratically. A passing, obviously experienced, policeman quickly assessed the situation: not enough petrol. He proved his point by successfully tilting it to one side and grinned at the smooth sound; a done deal. But they didn't supply the necessary adaptor connector to convert the outlet from 2-prong to 3-prong. So it was back to Wakil Electrics to do up a custom piece, which they managed to do in ten minutes. Then we remembered the Robertson bit; none of this would work without it. Fortunately, I had my Robertson screwdriver with me to use as an example of the bit profile. Deo had an idea; he knew a welding shop not far away that could cut off the front of my beloved screwdriver to use as the bit. Mission accomplished – all in one and a half hours.

Welder's fee: 3,000 shillings.

Adaptor cable: 15,000 shillings.

Wood drill bits: 20,000 shillings.

Extension cord: 54,000 shillings.

Electric Drill: 150,000 shillings.

Generator: 460,000 shillings.

The experience: Priceless.

I went to bed early after the hectic shopping spree, reflecting on how the Tanzanian framers would react to electrical power tools. The builders of both schools use hand tools for all of their work. I looked forward to showing off this new "modern" technology. Upon retiring, I set the alarm on my cell phone, reminding myself of Deo's early arrival at 6:00AM for the long drive out to Gongali.

At 4:00AM, a wet bed wakened me. No, my bladder wasn't the problem; the roof was leaking, profusely. I stepped out of bed, in pitch-black darkness, to an inch of water, and quickly leaped back up to the dry side of the mattress. It was interesting that the first thought I had was how to prevent electrocuting myself trying to turn on the lights. I felt my way across the bed and onto the bedside chair that connected me to my rubber-soled shoes in the closet. Standing on the chair, I put on my shoes and pants and passed under a premature shower on my way to the light switch.

A quick swipe of the switch and I could see the water pouring through the cracks in the ceiling plaster.

By the time Daniel, the duty receptionist who was sleeping on a cot behind the desk, sorted me out in a new room, Deo had arrived to pick me up. It would be a long day. Upon returning, I was told the story of the bursting water tank in the attic space above my room.

We had arranged to pick up Jacob along the way in Majengo. He had family in Karatu, and this was a good opportunity for a free ride to see them. Although Jacob and Mathew were both from the same Iraqw tribe (not to be confused with Iraqi, they pointed out), they had never met before the projects. Over the last few weeks, they had bumped into each other and were fast becoming good friends. They chatted non-stop for the first hour, exchanging stories from their youth.

At Karatu, after dropping Jacob off, Mathew and I met Philemon at the Paradise Restaurant where we poured over the list of materials remaining to be purchased. It checked out, so I handed over the last payment.

At the site, plastering of the exterior walls was well under way. It was a well coordinated process; one fellow "throwing" trowelfuls of mortar, evenly covering the wall with about three-quarters of an inch of mortar, followed by a leveler who screeded it with a straight length of wood to an even plane, followed by the finisher who steel-trowelled it to a smooth finish.

Applying cement plaster to seal the walls at Gongali school.

At the back of the building, digging of the two septic chambers was in progress: the first rectangular twelve-foot deep mixing chamber and the second round fifty-foot deep final chamber. Once finished, they would be lined with concrete blocks and plastered to a smooth finish. A sinewy-muscled man in each pit was hacking away at the red clay walls with the flat blade of a pick-axe, and then shoveling it out, unconcerned with the fine red dust blowing back in his face. Through a layer of settled dust on their backs, beads of sweat were carving pathways down the length of their long spines. From my point of view, it looked unbelievably exhausting in the sun, but each man's shift would go for hours. They were accustomed to the heat. I disregarded my

The next step is leveling the plaster to make it smooth.

previous concern about wall collapse; it would never happen since the compacted clay was as hard as concrete.

On top of the walls, the final sections of wood plates were being anchored to the lintel beam. This was a standard Canadian method that allowed the rafters to be easily and securely fixed, but it was a first for Fabian. The local method was to use lengths of wire set in the concrete lintel that could then be twisted over the rafters. Not a lasting or reliable solution in my mind, and fortunately, Fabian somewhat agreed. He was happy with the new "trick," and suggested a method of fixing the plates to the concrete beams using L-shaped rebar sections (my preferred threaded rod was not available) set in the concrete when wet. The vertical rebar

Nailing down the roof plates that will support the wooden trusses.

would extend up through holes drilled in the plates, then be bent over and nailed down with a couple of spikes at each location. That would work.

On a flat section of ground a distance from the building several carpenters were working quickly building trusses. They had already built two trusses.

"What the…?" I panicked to myself.

"Trusses?" I asked Mathew. "The plans show a post and beam layout."

No problem, Babu. I will tell Fabian he must change it."

We called a very anxious-looking Fabian over to discuss this potential major conflict.

"I am very sorry," Mathew translated. "But the carpenters want to do it traditional way. They are very experienced with work on Secondary Schools, and they do not understand your post and beam, and vaulted ceiling."

"But it is too late to change the design," I unconvincingly replied.

Two minutes later, I was working on the next truss with them. "Go with the flow, Al," I told myself. "There's something to be learned here."

The framers worked efficiently by placing rough-sawn two by four timber lengths on top of a completed truss, using it as a template. First the bottom chord, cut to the exact length of the width of the building, then the sloped rafters each side, extending a little extra in length, to be trimmed off later when in place using a string line, and finally the centre kingpost and two other vertical pieces, one on each side of the kingpost. All pieces were nailed, overlapping each other. The result was out-of-plane but that wouldn't matter; you would never be able to see it once the building was finished.

To speed things up, I set about building some trusses on my own, following their sample, with Mathew, Philemon and even Deo, happily pitching in to help.

Hammering together one of the many wooden trusses.

The wonderful atmosphere of productivity created a symphony of senses; the rhythmic sound of hand-sawing, the smell of sawdust floating in the breeze, the joking and laughter, interrupted by occasional short bursts of command from the foreman, the rat-tat-tat of driven spikes, and the lively coordinated bustle of muscle at work. Two men were selecting the right timber lengths from the pile and placing it on the template for the assemblers, while others were waiting to carry the finished trusses to the roof.

From the central breezeway, we passed finished trusses up to a couple of sure-footed young men standing on the lintel beams on

A completed wooden truss is being carried into place.

each side of the building, where they placed them temporarily, upside-down, and spaced evenly along the length of the walls.

It was never appropriate to unload the generator. I had already lost the war of the roof structure; there was no point in waging a battle of electric versus hand tools. It was later explained to me that the village did not want the generator for the simple reason that it was too much of a responsibility for them; they would have to put a twenty-four-hour guard on it, to protect it from theft or vandalism. ("Perhaps, down the road," I thought, "I could suggest a lockable storage enclosure of some sort.") In any case, I was enjoying the wonderfully basic physicality of hand-sawing rough timber and hammering spikes at their joints. It was good for the soul. The trusses were crudely built but they were strong and effective. I was content with the flat ceilings for the classrooms instead of the planned sloped ones.

The only interruption in the routine occurred right after a hearty meal of maize and beans, followed by some (tough to chew) chicken pieces. Several women who had been cleaning up started picking up pots and running with them to the storage shed, pointing to a wall of red dust in the distance. A dust storm was fast approaching. Fabian yelled at a few of the workers who quickly scrambled to weigh down the shed's loose sheet metal roofing with lengths of heavy timber.

It hit with a deafening roar. Its speed had to be approaching 60 miles per hour. Clouds of fine red clay dust swirled around the school walls and every other stationary object. Some people covered up their faces with their shirts; those who didn't, coughed. Some simply stood in place, leaning into the wind with their backs turned, waiting it out. Other hardier ones casually continued building trusses on the ground, their tee shirts billowing up to their armpits as they leaned over. The metal sheets on the shed roof rattled like fan-blown paper, but surprisingly, they held their own. Everyone's clothes were flapping; women's shawls and men's Maasai blankets were like flags flying furiously at half-mast.

Strangely, within five minutes, the wind had disappeared, leaving as quickly as it had arrived. It was fascinating.

Peter Hayshi, the district vice-chairman, showed up not long afterwards to add his token effort to the construction; though he helped lift some of the trusses onto the roof, the real purpose of his visit was to discuss the next phases of the project: "We will begin registration of the school, after the official opening on 9 December," he started. "But the Ministry of Education requires a teacher's residence to be in place before we use the school."

(That means another building project, I easily predicted.)

"Can you help us, Alan? We have a plan. The village will contribute 25% of its cost, if you can provide the rest. What we will do is negotiate with the government; by starting construction with our funds, we will show the government our commitment to build it, so that classes may be allowed to begin right away."

"We would love to help you," I said, "but funds may not be coming for six or eight months. It depends on the charity's success back in Canada."

"What about the plan for the residence?" I continued. "I could sketch out my ideas. The layout could have four or six rooms around shared kitchen and washroom...."

"No," he quickly but gently interrupted. "The standard government plan is for a building with rooms only. Village teachers prefer to cook traditionally, outdoors, with gathered wood for the open fire, in a fenced compound next to the building. We will use the government plan."

"And we cannot afford a separate septic tank," he continued, "they will use the visitor's toilets."

"And the cost?"

We discussed and concluded that twelve to thirteen million shillings would do it.

He wasn't finished. I vaguely remembered the very first meeting's discussion about the eventual need for three more buildings.

"We will need two more two-classroom buildings and an administration building," he said.

I suggested they could all be arranged around a central courtyard, where the children could play on grass, and flowers and small trees could be planted. He liked the idea.

"That may take many years to realize," I added.

"Yes, I know." He shrugged. "We can wait." And then, after shaking my hand as if to seal a deal, he left.

Although I was left a little flummoxed by Peter's assumptions about my commitment for these next phases, I didn't want to show any pessimism. In fact, it only made sense; the school would quickly outgrow its two classrooms in a year or so, and it could be fun to be involved in the "complete" project.

By late afternoon, it felt good to have built four of the sixteen trusses that were now on the roof, ready to be up-righted. Each end truss was stood up and braced in place and connected at the peak with a string line stretched across the length of the building to align the next trusses. There was just one more thing that needed discussion before we left; how to frame the dormers over the breezeway. After explaining the sequence of installing the ridge and valley beams, I climbed up on the lintel beams and worked with the carpenters to frame one side. Having had limited experience with dormer construction, they were content to follow my directions. It took until dark for us to complete the side.

While loading up to go, Deo agreed to give two workers a lift to Karatu. That was a mistake. The four of us had to get out repeatedly to give the car enough clearance to get over the many large bumps and ridges along the way. We picked up Jacob at Karatu. The rest of the three-hour ride to Arusha was long and tedious. It was nerve-racking for Deo, who had a few close calls with oncoming trucks creeping into our lane and playing the game of turning their blinding "brights" on at the last minute. Jacob and Mathew slept soundly; I couldn't.

ᕲᕲᕲ

The next day at Majengo we repeated sequence of activities that we had at Gongali. Only this time I got to use the generator and drill.

The weather had been holding out unbelievably well over the past few weeks. Since the deluge on November 15th, there had been no usually-expected rain. Goodluck at the Outpost glibly attributed it to global warming.

It was exciting to arrive and see how much progress had been made since the previous visit. At this point, Majengo advances matched the Gongali project; plasterers were hurling their mortar at the walls, a few workers, women as well as men, were forming up the large ten-foot-diameter concrete cover for the septic pit, and the three carpenter roof framers, Grason, Ali and Ali (they enjoyed the confusion at times of two same names) were installing the ridge beams along the length of the building. They had been anxiously awaiting my arrival so that the next stage of rafter framing could be discussed.

I was impressed with the butt-joining details of the ridge beam, a process where two lengths of timber are spliced together to form one long piece. Ali and Ali, both recent young graduates of the local Vocational Training Centre, proudly demonstrated their skills. The joint, an elongated "zee"-shape, although time-consuming to build, was perfect. To their smiles, my photo taking acknowledged it.

The discussion with Jacob and Hemedi was quick. I agreed to compromise on the number of rafters as well as the need to notch the rafters onto the ridge beam and lintel plate. An angled butt joint would be OK. So I strapped on my tool belt and went to work to help with the framing.

The first task was to fix the wood lintel plates to the concrete lintel beam. Hemedi assigned me to be the "measurer"; to measure the distances of the vertical bolts embedded in the concrete, and mark up the wood plates accordingly, so matching holes could be drilled, and hopefully the plates would be installed with the holes coinciding with the bolt locations. I followed the old carpenter adage "measure twice and cut once," and the results were generally good.

We used the generator to power the hole drilling. Neither Hemedi nor anyone else at the site had used one in construction before. When we took it out of the box, everyone stopped work and stared at Jacob as he was about to pull the rip chord. It started on the first pull, its efficient four-stroke humming and vibrating beautifully, true to its Japanese quality standards.

The sound of the generator attracted the attention of a number of curious four- to ten-year-old neighborhood kids. Gathered in a semi-circle around the drilling, they silently watched as I drilled in a safe area away from the building. *Why not let them experience it?* I thought. I beckoned the closest older boy and motioned for him to grab the handle and squeeze the trigger.

I aligned the bit with the hole and held the body of the drill to steady it. Wide-eyed and excited, he firmly wrapped his two little hands around the handle and nervously squeezed. I guess he didn't

Alan drilling roof plates with the new generator at the Majengo site.

understand that when the hole was drilled, he should let go of the trigger. The rest of the kids broke into raucous laughter at the look of fear on his face; he was afraid to let go as the drill rattled around in the hole. I wrestled the drill from his hand, told him it was OK, and offered him another try at the next hole. He did well on his attempt, and so did the next child, and on it went, all the other kids crowding in now for a turn.

What fun I had with them, giving them each a try, but I wondered if it would be the last time in their lives some would get to hold a power tool.

Once the plates were bolted down, we selected the best timbers for the rafters and cut the proper angle at the head and left extra length at the bottom for final trimming when all were in place. Halfway through the rafter work, Jacob insisted I join the workers for a local pub lunch.

We walked for about ten or fifteen minutes through the typical "in-streets" of this large crowded district. I was apparently an amusing sight; I had forgotten to take off my tool belt and the jingle-jangle of hammer and tools were drawing curious looks from the locals.

The walk was an eye-opener.

We always accessed Teddy's project by driving around the perimeter of Majengo to her home in the southern end, close to a forested area. I had never been "up close and personal" with the more depressed living conditions that I now saw as we made our way through a maze of narrow passageways in the inner areas between the "main" roads of the district.

Many of the small one-room homes were made of the traditional rural wattle-and-daub wall construction with thatched roofs, but on some walls, the rain had crumbled away the mud aggregate, leaving holes that no-one seemed interested in repairing – or perhaps, was able to repair, for that matter. Women were cooking outside their home's entrance on the uneven ground surface using either kerosene stoves, or charcoal and wood branches, for heating.

"Where do they get the charcoal?" I asked.

"There is a business that uses cut hardwood from the forests," Jacob said. "They burn large amounts of cut-up timber and sell the charcoal product."

On one corner, a couple of women were cleaning a large pot of sardine-sized fish, getting them ready to dry on racks in the sun.

"They will sell that to the shops," Jacob explained.

We passed a large dirt playing field that was multifunctional; the grass around its perimeter was covered with clothes drying in the sun and at the far end, the city provided a large trailerable water tank for public use. A line of women and children, some as young as four or five, streamed past us, carrying 5-gallon plastic containers of water balanced on their heads in their sure-footed and inimitable "no-hands" style.

I recalled Teddy's water tap in her yard. "So how did Teddy manage to have water piped to her yard?" I asked.

"She was lucky," Jacob said. "Her street is one of the few to have underground piping."

"The city tank is a community focal point," Jacob continued. "They fetch water and also do their laundry there. Mothers are happy now that school is out so children can help with the chores."

The human density was astounding. We passed more than a hundred people in our short walk. I imagined how dispiriting it must be to local building and health officials who are trying to provide solutions aimed at combating the overwhelming conditions.

"Jacob, how many people in this district?"

"We don't know exactly, because the government is lacking in census taking. I think there must be over 50,000 people here, and the population is growing."

Despite their hardships, I witnessed in their daily routine a quiet acceptance of their lifestyle. They went about their daily regimen with communal conviviality; neighbors chatting and laughing as they prepared outdoor meals within conversation distance of each other; children happily playing with crude but functional toys on whatever level compacted clay surface was available nearby their home; shopkeepers selling confectionery, pop, and miscellaneous small household items stuffed into their converted one-room homes.

And there were no beggars or street persons, as we know them it in the western world. The community took responsibility. Neighbours like Teddy that had any little spare space whatsoever took the orphans in and cared for them. They did not appear despondent or miserable; instead, I sensed a strong will to keep going, one day at a time.

No better was this will demonstrated than in the local Majengo gravel-making business, an excellent example of the laws of supply and demand. The yards supplying machine–made gravel, where large stones are mechanically reduced to the various sizes for concrete aggregate, are located some distance away. Local Majengo builders typically build with a lot of concrete, so they use a lot of gravel. They can't afford the machine-made stuff because the material is expensive plus they pay additional trucking charges.

Some enterprising individuals in the community had come up with an alternative plan. Microbusinesses. Builders would deposit small truckloads of boulders in available open spaces around the perimeter of the district, to be purchased mostly by single parent women for about 10,000 shillings a load. After about a month of hammering and chiseling the boulders into small pieces, the women would get paid 20,000 shillings by the builders for each small truckload of gravel. Small children worked alongside mothers. The work was painstakingly repetitive and extremely daunting, but the income (Cdn$7.14) was enough to help support the family with the basic necessities: rice, milk, maize, vegetables.

I was impressed when Jacob explained how the community controlled fairness of sales among the women. Builders had to go through a community-appointed "chairman" to ensure their purchases were rotated through the different businesses. To avoid the

Microbusiness at Majengo – breaking stones, by hand, into gravel.

temptation for corruption, the appointment of the "chairman" was changed every month.

Although it was difficult to see the families toiling this way, I had to be thankful for the cheaper gravel; it was a significant factor in reducing costs for the project.

We arrived at the local pub, a simple building with several small, dimly-lit, one-window rooms, furnished with plastic tables and chairs. It was busy. The kitchen prepared their only menu item, skewered beef or goat, french-fries and cabbage and onion salad, in a tiny alcove near the entrance. The young teenage chef worked efficiently in the corner, alternating between the meat cooking on a metal grate on a charcoal-filled metal box, and the sizzling fries in a wok balanced on a small charcoal-filled drum on the floor. The red-hot embers of both stoves produced vivid gradations of black, red, orange and yellow on the adjacent wall. The only waitress working there multi-tasked as receptionist, server and cashier.

We ate heartily, with little concern for cholesterol content, enjoying good-natured banter and some merry hat swapping.

Not long after returning to the site, Cosmas approached me. With a smiling twinkle in his eye, he motioned me to join him and Teddy for a surprise treat. They had spent a couple of hours preparing a large feast for me, and were unaware that I had been to the pub. I wasn't about to spoil the party; it dawned on me that they must have felt that this was the last opportunity for a grand gesture of appreciation. I then recalled Teddy and one of the single mothers huddled, peeling vegetables, cooking, in the corner room of their house when I had earlier peeked in looking for my misplaced briefcase.

They pulled out all the stops on the menu selection: pan-fried fish, rice with peas, carrots, plantain, boiled potatoes, and for dessert, pineapple and sliced apple. For drinks, they offered the house special; Sprite or Coca-Cola. I ate as heartily as I was able and was surprised how comfortable and enjoyable the conversations were, despite their stilted but valiant English. When I stepped outside to go back to work, I was content in the knowledge of the satisfaction that Teddy and Cosmas would have felt; it surpassed the pain of my bloated stomach.

A lot was accomplished in the remaining few hours of the day; the septic cover concreting, the plastering and the roof framing.

Jacob pointed out that it was Hemedi's wife, Mama Aziza, who was the main force in the concreting activity. She was an incredible sight to behold; a short, heavy-set, large-breasted woman in her African patterned long skirt, rolled up sleeved sweater, and wool toque, mixing the concrete ingredients on the ground and shoveling it into the formwork with such energy and strength. The concrete mud soaking her shoes and socks and splashing her skirt did not concern her. She was determined to finish the concreting before the end of the day.

It was hard to understand that Mama Aziza didn't have a sore back, the way it was bent forward at such an impossible angle with her behind permanently pointed upward. Her helper was the opposite; a beautiful tall slim almost-too-elegantly-dressed young woman in a long gold-coloured skirt, a pristine white blouse and delicate fabric head wrap. She appeared a little out of place, and fueled by a different determination, not to get any concrete on her clothes. She gingerly passed buckets of sand and gravel to Mama Aziza, and stood well back of the shoveling.

The rest of the rafters went very quickly. Like at Gongali, I enjoyed sawing the timbers with the capable new Irwin saw I had purchased back in Canada just for the project, and then hammering them into place. And fortunately, there was just enough daylight remaining for me to help the carpenters with the tricky framing of the entrance dormer.

Hemedi's wife Aziza – working hard while in charge of concrete.

I always feel a kinship with anyone that enjoys working with wood, as I do; like my two stepsons, Stephen and Jeffrey Miller. Stephen is an amazing craftsman who balances his professional joinery trade with the marvelously exacting hobby of marquetry, and Jeff has been enjoying building his own wood-framed home that proudly displays some excellently crafted wood detailing.

These African framers had a great sense of humour. The antics that had started at the pub continued up in the roof rafters, much to the delight of the street kids below. They laughed heartily at the staged mock fight we posed for the camera, with me holding my hammer over Ali's head, and Ali with his (my) saw at my throat.

Alan, carpenter Ali and other workers joking around during roof-framing at the Majengo site.

It was a great day that culminated in a lovely surprise; a dozen kids rushed me, crowding around to say goodbye with high fives and hugs. A little one held onto my leg – for the longest time.

It was dark when we left the site. The drive through the main Majengo street was surreal. In the absence of streetlights, the hundreds of locals and returning commuters, walking, sitting, leaning against doorways, appeared as eerie shadows, their figures in front of us silhouetted by oncoming headlights that highlighted the ever-present floating dust.

The two days of construction at the sites on November 30 and December 1 were great. Construction issues were all sorted out with the builders, so it was clear sailing in the next week to the construction completion celebrations.

᠄ᢣᢣ᠄

Mathew visited the site by himself on Sunday, December 5, to review and report on the work of the past few days, but also to deliver the generator that Philemon had requested for the sound system they were going to rent. I stayed behind to catch up on typing and e-mails.

I knew both owners were planning an interesting agenda, but they weren't letting me in on the details. Apart from the presentation of Esther's gifts, I didn't know what exactly was expected of me. I did suggest to Mathew that it would be a wonderful charity fund-raising tool to have a video of school children singing, perhaps with a message in English, similar to the performances at Teddy's Majengo classes last week.

Mathew phoned on Monday morning to brief me on his visit, and to confirm dinner with his family that evening. I took the opportunity to ask about Gongali, "So how about some more details. Is there an agenda yet?"

"Philemon is planning a big celebration for everyone in the village area," he said. "All I know is there will be the children doing something special for you; the women have something planned and the elders as well."

"How many?" I asked.

"Maybe two hundred to three hundred people," Mathew said.

"That many? Incredible… and special guests?"

"Lazarus Titus, the district chairman, Peter Hayshi, vice-chairman, Philemon, of course, and the district education officer…."

"That's good. We need to discuss registration of the school with him. What about speeches? Am I expected to…."

"Up to you."

"Hmmmm… can you translate for me as I speak? [*What am I doing? It's my biggest fear.*]"

"Hakuna matata, babu Alan."

"So, what time for dinner tonight?" I asked. "I hope Rose isn't spending a lot of time and energy on a big meal. She must be still recovering."

"She has been working all day on it, with the help of her friend Mary, and Lissa, of course."

"And how's little Maureen? I can't wait to see her."

"She's fine. We're not getting much sleep though."

The evening spent at Mathew's home was very pleasant. The Sulles are a typical middle class family. They are considered well off, but like their Canadian counterparts, both parents work to maintain their desired standard of living. Rose works as a receptionist at a local hotel.

The star attraction, of course, was seeing little Maureen: with the big beautiful eyes of her mother and Lissa. It was a treat to see an African newborn baby for the first time. She will no doubt inherit the intelligence of her parents, as Lissa did. I asked Lissa how school was going, which prompted Rose to bring out her final report card from her English Medium Pre-School. Her marks were an unbelievable 98%. She ranked number 1 in her class of 42.

The biggest impression Lissa made on me was with her English-speaking ability at such a young age. Tanzanian children have the option to attend either an English Medium School or a regular Swahili school. The Tanzanian government apparently has mandated learning of the English language as an important step in furthering the country's economic development.

Fortunately, I had brought along my laptop computer to download Mathew's photos from the previous day's site visit (progress was good; everything was on track for the 9th). Lissa's eyes widened at the sight of it as she huddled next to me, eager to witness the wonders of the computer. I demonstrated the various programs, from drawing to typing to Internet use. It was fun teaching her to type for the first time; back and forth, I typed questions that she answered, in hesitant but passable English.

CHAPTER 7

CELEBRATIONS

"The curious beauty of African music is
that it uplifts even as it tells a sad tale."

– NELSON MANDELA

Energetic and joyous dance celebrations at Gongali.

Thursday, December 9, arrived very quickly: the big day at Gongali. I was a little nervous but excited. The weather was holding out, still no rain, a little breeze, cloudy, perfect conditions for the celebrations.

At Karatu, we stopped for coffee. Mathew got excited seeing an elderly man at the next table. I was introduced to a tall, solidly-built, handsome seventy-year-old with a youthful smile and an air of worldliness. He was an important and famous man in Mathew's village, a retired farmer who was reputed to have single-handedly killed a lion in his youth.

On the trail from Karatu to Gongali, a speeding jeep passed us, almost running us off the road.

"What the hell—" I shouted.

"Ha ha ha," Mathew chortled. "That was Peter. He probably forgot to buy something and is rushing to pick it up in Karatu."

We were on a small rise still two or three miles from the school when Mathew pointed the school out in the distance. All one could see was a sliver of shiny silver; the reflection of the sun on the sheet metal roof. I reflected also on the last four weeks, and how much had been accomplished on both projects. Regardless of the deadline we imposed, because of both my scheduling and the approaching rains, the builders had been motivated by a strong passion well beyond their norm. They well understood the significance of the school and its value not only to the community, but more tangibly, to their family. It explained why so many had come up to personally thank me.

We arrived at the site to a hubbub of activity. The range of emotions I experienced in the next few hours cannot be adequately described. Fabian and Philemon, in their usual quiet manner, greeted me with big smiles. We walked among the villagers for a few moments and had a quick look inside the new school before the official start of events. Scattered around the area were hundreds of men, women and children of all ages, from many miles away, all belonging to the Iraqw tribe. Almost all of them had walked to get here. They were dressed in their best, the women as usual outdoing the men with their colourful dresses and headwraps.

There were many tribal elders clothed in their traditional blankets, with their herding sticks a permanent part of their attire, and with their uniquely-crafted rubber tire shoes. I caught glimpses of several groups of villagers at the back of the building rehearsing songs, dances and drumming performances. Mathew was surprised to see two of his former primary school teachers, whom he hadn't seen since 1986.

To the side of the building a large tarpaulin covered the roof and walls of a well-made temporary post and beam structure crafted from branches of the *minyaa* tree. Inside, tables and chairs were lined along the back wall, facing the open wall in front. This was the area designated for the official gathering.

The building was nearly complete; the roof was on, fascia boards had been painted, plastering was complete, the plaster blackboards had been roughed in, and one of the exterior walls had been painted in the colour Philemon and I had chosen to complement that of the rich, warm tones of the red clay. The builders were still working, installing ceiling boards. They hooted in excitement when they saw me, remembering our time together last week, and invited me to nail a few panels with them. I did a few token nailings. In a week the building would be totally completed. The only things left to do were the door installations, the fitting of the glass into the window frames, the plumbing fixtures installations, and to paint, paint, paint.

Philemon then led me to the head table to sit with district chairman Lazarus Titus, district vice-chairman Peter Hayshi, the district education officer, and Philemon. The villagers gathered inside, around the perimeter of the tented enclosure, tightly packed shoulder to shoulder, the little children sitting in front, leaving a large open space in front of our tables.

Peter, who had passed us on the road, had hurriedly returned from Karatu with a rented microphone and sound system that could be powered using the new generator. It was set up just in time, and then, prompted by a lively emcee personality, the speeches began. First Peter, then Lazarus, then a touching tribute from a man, then a woman, each representing the male and female voices of the community. When they had finished, they presented me with their English written words.

Then it was my turn. I had spent the previous two days practicing my speech that Goodluck at the Outpost had translated for me. It was a little jilted, but I got through it. I followed the routine of the previous speeches; say a line and wait for the cheering and clapping to end. The boisterous crowd was responding with their traditional cry of jubilation, a high-pitched warble (that I found difficult to later emulate). My final line:

"Natumaini nitarudi upesi kwa mara nyingine kuwaona, na pia kukutana na watahiniwa wa baadaye wa shule yenu."

["I hope to come back to see you again, and especially in the future, to meet the graduates of this school."]

After my speech, I presented Esther's gift to Lazarus, and called Fabian forward to give him the gift of my trusty 26-foot tape measure he had so admired when we had worked together.

Then it was time for the entertainment. I was in awe of the three once-in-a-lifetime performances that followed.

The first was performed by a group of about 50 children in two long lines that entered through a parted opening in the crowd. Circling in front of me, they sang and danced to the rhythm of one drummer beating on a homemade, skin-covered, shallow wooden drum. Their rehearsed English lines, repeated many times, gave me pleasure yet again:

"We are enjoy; we are so happy (sung by a single child)

We are enjoy, today we are so happy (the chorus)."

An impressively sung and danced Swahili song followed the English performance.

The second performance was incredibly moving; about 26 men and women entered in two lines and formed in front of us, the women in the front row, the men in the back. A drummer off to the side clicked a few beats to start off the singing; a very slow rhythmical Swahili song that thanked me for the gift to their community; the movements instinctual, sensual and graceful, their bodies bent forward (to show respect, I was told), swaying gently from side to side, their shoulders and hands raising and "pushing" down, as if to calm the earth, stepping forward a few steps, then back a few steps, all in impressive unison. The women voiced the words in a sweet pitch; the men provided a rich baritone and bass background chant: unbelievably beautiful.

The final performance was more dynamic and robust, and dusty. It was the way they celebrated special occasions; a ring of hardy men jumping Maasai-style, shouting to the beat of every jump around seated women beating furiously on a large shallow, skin-covered drum, their voices visceral, powerful – a muscular sound whooshing from the depths of their lungs with every jump – but with clouds of fine red dust rising from every heavy landing, eventually shrouding their performance and choking us to the point where the emcee put a stop to it. I didn't really mind; it was a rare and fascinating treat.

When the dust settled, it was time for the presentations. I should have guessed what they had in store for me. "Babu Mkubwa" Alan was to be transformed into a village elder. I was wrapped in a traditional Maasai blanket, given a pair of hand-made ceremonial (rubber tire) shoes and presented with a herding stick. Then Philemon's wife Anna approached me and put her arms around me, but when I tried to return her "hug", she quickly drew back, "Babu, I'm trying to give you a present."

Alan's formal initiation as an honourary elder with the donning of the traditional Maasai blanket.

She continued, wrapping me in yet another Maasai blanket. "This is for your wife."

"Ahsante," I thanked her sheepishly.

To the loud cheers of the surrounding villagers, I was led away to one of the new classrooms for yet another amazing event.

Inside the room, all the village elders (about 30 to 35) had gathered. They were sitting on the floor around a large cauldron of a greyish bubbling brew called "busa," a local mixture of maize flour, millet and sorghum, fermented for a few days, to produce a high alcohol content concoction that would be ceremoniously passed around and drunk by everyone. Surprisingly, a handful of elderly women sat in a corner of the room. Outside, curious villagers piled up against the security grating of the two open windows on each side of the room, the metal frames providing a silent portrait of interesting faces.

A chair was arranged for me in the centre, where I sat and awaited my fate; I was to be initiated as an elder. With a large wooden bowl, a senior "babu" scooped a portion from the vat and placed it under my chin. It tasted OK, although a little vinegary and gritty. There was loud chatter and animated discussion. After everyone drank (some considerably more than the norm), the highest ranking in the community stood up and with outstretched arms, called for silence. It took several minutes to calm them. He then proceeded with the praying part. For at least a half hour, he repeatedly chanted several lines at a time, to which the group responded with "hie" [amen], spoken in a low powerfully resonant whisper. The room was alive, pulsating with the rhythm of the "hie's" repeated at the pace of normal human breathing. I felt both honored and humbled by the significance and extraordinariness of what was happening.

After the initiation, we feasted in the other classroom on rice pilau, roast goat and pineapple, and drank South African merlot.

Alan's initiation as an honourary elder involved drinking "busa."

At one point, I leaned over to Lazarus sitting next to me and asked, "What are the district's highest priorities?"

"Education, water and health," he quickly replied.

"Is there a fourth and a fifth?" I asked.

"We have enough on our hands with these three," he replied dryly.

"Water… hmmmm. What Claude Goi did with his piped water system from the mountain stream was amazing, wasn't it?"

"Yes, but we need more solutions."

"Such as?"

"Drilling is the only effective method. But it's costly, and expensive, and risky. You have to drill down at least 150 to 200 feet in this area to get water. Without government funds, we rely on private contractors to drill, at the owner's expense. It costs about US$10,000 for each hole, and you pay whether they find water or not."

That reminded me of my nephew David Van Wyck's property on BC's Gabriola Island, where he searched in vain for water, and gave up after several drilling failures. Ironically, his neighbour succeeded on his first try. David had to resort to purchasing water and storing it in a large plastic container. I mused also at the memory of my visit there at the time, when his father Bill, my brother-in-law and retired Manitoba farmer, sporadically and optimistically walked the property with his dowsing rod, but only to confirm without any doubt, at least in his mind, that a water source on David's property was nowhere to be found.

"That reminds me," I continued. "On the way here, I noticed

two cows harnessed to a cart, pulling a large plastic container of water, but with no-one around to lead them. What happened?"

Lazarus laughed. "The cows are trained to find their way home from Claude's watering hole. The farmers have several carts. It takes so long to fill from the dribbling tap that they send a filled one on home while they wait for the next one to fill."

"Ingenious!"

Four hours after we arrived, it was over. We took our time with long good-byes, photo-taking and hand shakes with the scores of villagers, kids and adults alike. A couple of dozen children surrounded me with their arms outstretched, some restrained by their mothers, innocently and unabashedly reaching up for my head. I recognized the previous experience with Jacob's children who were fascinated with my hair. I couldn't deny them. As I bent forward giving permission, they charged, laughing and giggling, their mothers trying to control them as they playfully messed my mane. Mathew, sensing I needed to be rescued, managed to pull me away, and led me to the taxi. We drove slowly away, smiling at the few young boys running alongside, trying to keep up as long as they could.

I was still overwhelmed as I sat in silence on the drive back to Arusha, reflecting; how lucky I was to have had this experience. And how important education was to the community. Exhausted, I fell asleep, with images of the dozens of innocent-faced children to remember, varying from the friendliest and boisterous to the shy bewildered wide-eyed little toddlers who had yet to understand the events of the day.

Saying goodbye after the Gongali school opening celebrations.

The next day, Pineal Mero, the Little Stars headmaster, arranged to take us to the local office of the Ministry of Education and Vocational Training, the key connection I needed, to obtain all the required information and forms for designing and building schools. Godwin Elisa from the bank had offered to be involved with my projects. He explained that it was his "corporate responsibility" to help, so I invited him along. The meeting revealed, as expected, a bureaucratically tedious process involving a lot of form-filling and circulation through various levels of government. Mr. Victor Bwindiki, the chief building inspector for the Arusha/ Manyara Zone, gave us all the required paperwork, thanked me for the contributions to his country, and offered to help in any way he could to make the process as smooth as possible. Great! I was relieved for that.

ᗱᢥᣟ

Saturday, 11 December; the day for the official construction completion celebration at the Majengo site had arrived. I invited Godwin Elisa and his wife Neema. We arrived to see about 50 children and a handful of invited guests, mainly Teddy's teachers and relatives, patiently awaiting our arrival. They were seated under a large canopy erected in the open space between Teddy's home and the new school, the sunshine producing a reddish brown glow on everyone's skin through the canopy's translucent orange fabric.

The carpenter crew members, Grason, Ali and Ali, were still putting the finishing touches on the building, installing window glass, painting and doing minor touch-ups to the plaster. I was suitably impressed. The craftsmanship of the finished roofing, plastering, fascia and trim was excellent. The only work left to finish was the painting, installation of washroom fixtures, and application of the final cement veneer floor finish.

Once seated, Cosmas's brother led us through an opening prayer that was followed by a wonderfully warm and informative dialogue from Teddy. With Godwin sitting next to me providing a running translation, she explained the history of her home's mini orphanage, and the single mothers she had been accommodating there, and how the new school and craft centre would be their ticket to a better life. A well-rehearsed song sung for me by 30 or 40 children followed that.

And then came my speech and my presentation of Esther's and Hemedi's gifts; almost an exact repeat of what I did at Gongali, except my Swahili word pronunciations were improving.

The next event was a first for me: the official school ribbon-cutting, accompanied by great clapping and boisterous cheers and whistles as I spent a minute or two struggling with dull scissors.

The completed ten-foot-diameter septic tank concrete cover located in the centre of the yard proved to have wonderful cere-monial value. The children were summoned to place themselves in a ring around it. They danced and sang, circling around and around, while one of the teachers in the centre prompted them with the words. A talented young girl with a whistle and a plastic pail as a drum provided the music accompaniment. It was joyous and fun for both kids and teachers. Even the workers stopped working during the performance and clapped and cheered to the strong rhythms of the drum.

Everyone, especially the young children, enjoyed a hearty meal of tilapia, beef, rice pilau, carrot and cabbage salad prepared in one of the tiny single women's rooms. By now, I had become used to the Tanzanian custom of eating with my fingers. I was no longer self-conscious; in fact, it felt natural, and efficient. It is amazing how much easier it is to pick out fish bones with your fingers than with a knife and fork. And I like the ceremony of having someone come around to each person, before and after the meal, with soap and a bowl of water to wash your hands.

As the final item on the agenda, Teddy presented gifts: an attractive tablecloth and place mats, finely embroidered, handcrafted by the locals as an example of what the Crafts Room would be producing to sell at the Central Market, and a large heart-shaped cake to be enjoyed by everyone. The kids' eyes lit up when it was proudly brought out.

The cake was cut up into small bite-size squares, and I was surprised at their interesting tradition of feeding each other the pieces.

Orphan children at the new Majengo school opening celebrations.

The finished school at Majengo coated in yellow stucco.

Teddy fed Godwin, Neema, Jacob, the teachers, relatives, and me; Cosmas fed Teddy, and I was invited to feed the children. So one mouth at a time, I got to enjoy all the different little personalities as they opened wide for me, some voraciously gobbling the piece down in one gulp, others taking it from me to savour more slowly. What a great experience it was. Later, Jacob explained to me that the reason for this tradition involving the adults was to celebrate friendship, and to show respect. But with the children, it was to help them to remember their elders, and more pointedly, the one that fed them.

Three short hours after arriving, it was over. The children were dismissed. We said goodbye to the teachers and relatives, and they left. Teddy and I agreed to "keep in touch" through Jacob, since

I wanted to follow up with possible future assistance for school supplies and equipment as well as be provided with reports on the school's operation. Our good-byes were very heartfelt. I didn't know if I would see this amazing person again, but I knew that with her strength and determination and the community's support, the school would survive. Her resolve was demonstrated quite emphatically when she looked at me warmly and with a big smile, announced her final words (in carefully phrased English), "I will take English lessons now."

***

I awoke Sunday morning and decided it would be a day of reflection and rest as well as an opportunity to record the details of the extraordinary experiences at both schools' celebrations. I was also eager for the morning walk that I'd had to forgo for a few days, so I quickly dressed and headed out the main gate of the lodge and up Serengeti Road.

I felt great; life was good; I was cheery with everyone along the way. Church-going pedestrians were all so well-dressed and friendly. As a bonus, because it was Sunday, traffic was at a minimum, and the usual "running the gauntlet" crossing through bumper-to-bumper, fume-filled traffic of Old Moshi Road had become a relaxing stroll.

On the other side, heading up Hailie Selassie Road, I noticed a young man in a stained T-shirt and jeans ahead of me, struggling to push one of those commonly seen home-made wooden carts up the slight incline, probably headed toward the fruit stands at the next intersection. He was sweating profusely; these carts are heavy. The floor and sides are made from thick planks of lumber and are supported by wheels and axles scavenged from abandoned cars. A thick beam attached to the sides extended out equally to the front and back to a cross bar at each end. Nailed to the front cross bar are strips of rubber tires that act as brakes. You push from the back bar. I was in such a good mood, I sidled up along side the young fellow and joined his effort.

"Jambo," I greeted.

"Jambo," he returned, and immediately stepped aside, pulled out his cell-phone and proceeded to chat away, leaving me to struggle on my own.

It took a few hundred yards for my enthusiasm to wane. I dropped the bar; I was spent. Despite my Sunday best being now drenched in sweat, I smiled at him, shrugged my shoulders, and left, chuckling at the comedy of it all, especially since I had noticed that the produce cart was empty; a "fruitless" effort to say the least. It surely was an interesting departure from the intense co-operation I had experienced with the school work crews.

My walk routine had developed another interesting aspect; my relationship with two street cleaning women. Every day, while being passed unnoticed by hundreds of pedestrian commuters, they dutifully swept the dirt trails that acted as sidewalks on either side of the paved road. With absolute minimum pay, they were probably eking out an existence. They worked at different points along my walk.

One was particularly sad looking, stooped, humpbacked and very old. She moved slowly but deliberately, sweeping wind-stormed leaves and twigs off the trail. I wanted to be discreet in offering her a few shillings, so I walked up to her with a two-thou-sand-shilling note wedged between my thumb and palm and shook her hand, expecting her to close her fingers on it. But perhaps stupefied by my enthusiastic handshake, she wasn't aware of the note, so I gently cupped her fingers over it. She looked at the note, then up at me, in somewhat disbelief. I walked away, smiling, while she continued her expressionless stare.

The other woman further down the road was middle-aged and colourful. She always offered a slight smile as I passed and I would always respond with "Leo, una mapendesa." [Today, you look very beautiful.] Despite the drudgery of her work, she always dressed in brightly-coloured skirts and head wraps. I did the same handshake maneuver with her, but her surprise was only fleeting. She understood what was happening.

I had continued this routine almost every day for the last two weeks of my stay. Every day after the first meeting, I saw a brief pause in their sweeping as they noticed me approaching from a distance. On my last strolling, I said my final goodbye in the best Swahili I could muster. They smiled and seemed to understand my sadness.

❧

The last few days in Arusha had some interesting developments.

On Monday, Deo drove Jacob and me to the village of Kikatiki, about 12 miles from Arusha on the Moshi Road, where Andrew Titus had previously arranged for us to tour his community vocational and school project, and then to look at his acreage property, the site of his new school proposal. The Kikatiki Vocational Center, although still a work in progress, was very impressive nonetheless. Andrew's son Joachim managed the collection of six or seven small buildings that housed classrooms, a welding workshop, a sewing room, bunkroom accommodation for 20 orphans, and a tiny dining/cooking building.

But financially, the centre was just barely getting by. A modest income derived from the sale of farm crops, and marketable items produced by the welding and sewing classes, such as steel bunk beds, chairs, window security grates, steel doors and clothing, helped to offset the centre's operating and maintenance costs. I was impressed with Andrew's ingenious design of rainwater collection. Roof water, from gutters and pipes on several buildings, was stored in a large, underground, concrete tank, but the pump to distribute it to plumbing fixtures hadn't been working for some time. There was no money to fix it. And since Andrew was running the centre on a shoestring budget, there were certainly no spare funds for him to realize his dream of opening a new much-needed primary school.

The school was definitely needed; when we stopped along the road just before reaching the village to take pictures of a wonderful panoramic view of Mount Kilimanjaro, a woman walking towards us carrying a large bundle of papers, greeted us with a very friendly smile. I had an idea.

"Jacob, ask her about the school situation in the area," I said.

We were in luck.

"I am a nursery school teacher," she explained. "There are no primary schools to serve our immediate area; the nearest ones are too far and transportation is difficult."

It wasn't that I doubted Andrew's assessment, but a second opinion was always helpful.

After our tour of the centre, we drove to the proposed site over a mile off the highway down a dirt road, passing several small adobe brick homes. Not far from each home was an abandoned kiln next to a large excavated pit.

"Why so many kilns?" I queried Andrew.

"It's the most economical way to build. Each homeowner excavates the clay from his property and builds his own small kiln to fire the bricks. It works well. I'm not happy with the scars it leaves on the landscape, but they do not have the funds or the inclination to fill the pits in."

The two- to three-acre site was almost ideally located, within range of many homes that we could see in the area. The land was a little sloped, but workable. There were scattered trees and a few rock features that Andrew wanted to highlight, but the most impressive feature was the views. To the north was a clear view of

With Andrew Titus at another proposed school site.

Mount Kilimanjaro; to the west, Mount Meru, and to the south, the hills where the relatively new and popular mineral, tanzanite, was mined. Sounded like a good candidate for the next new school.

I met Mr. Liberty Kinabo on my morning walk the next day. He was a trade officer for the Tanzanian government, responsible for liaising with local businesses to resolve economic issues and improve public/private sector relationships. Liberty had a personal project, to build a school in his Kilimanjaro home region, and, as one would guess, he was just waiting for a funding plan. We exchanged e-mails for future reference.

Pineal Mero dropped in to the Outpost Lodge in the afternoon to discuss his project: a new school in the village of Babati, south of Karatu, at about the same distance from Arusha as Karatu.

It just seemed remarkable how often the subject of education surfaced with almost everyone I met. Everyone was aware of the need, and certainly, among the intelligentsia, there seemed to be a realization that since Tanzanians cannot rely on government action alone, they must take personal action.

🔅

On Tuesday evening, my last night in Tanzania, I celebrated by inviting the "team" out to dinner at Albero's (seems like they misspelled Alberto's), a good local Italian restaurant. Jacob, his wife Birgita, Mathew and Rose, Godwin and Neema, Deogratius and Magdelena, had all contributed in invaluable ways to the projects' success. As I pointed out in my speech to them, they were the ones who had done all the work; I had just followed their lead.

The most important reason for the dinner was to get them to meet and learn each other's roles for future projects. It seemed like they were a good team; Godwin, excellent English, bank officer, with his own internet-connected computer, would be my main contact. Mathew would continue on with the next phases of Gongali, where the teacher's residence was urgently needed. Jacob would look after the next new project. And Deo, thankful for the project's earnings, would be looking forward to upgrading to a 4-wheel drive to keep us out of the muddy clay.

I toasted Jacob and Mathew, Jacob for initiating this adventure during an innocent conversation that we'd had during our descent off Mount Kilimanjaro back in September, and both Mathew and Jacob, for their commitment and love of their family and community. Little had they known at the beginning of this adventure that the result would be the building of two durable schools and a strengthening of the friendship between us.

The good-byes were heartfelt. After having shared their lives for five weeks now, these Tanzanians were like family to me. Their parting words were unforgettable: "Don't forget Tanzania. We need you."

"Don't worry, I'll be back," I said, "and hopefully my wife will be willing and able to join me."

CHAPTER 8

A Promise To Return

"We make a living by what we get,
but we make a life by what we give."

– WINSTON CHURCHILL

Children in front of their new classrooms at the finished Gongali school.

Sitting in the Schiphol terminus in Amsterdam, on the way home, I reflected on how quickly the last few weeks had gone by, and how much had been accomplished in such a short time. We had built two schools in five weeks, and it had been easier than I expected. The next ones would be even easier, with the "team" in place, and my having figured out the protocols and procedures with the Ministry of Education.

I admit that my approach was naïve and unorthodox: going to a strange country, armed with nothing but a pocket full of cash and a couple of promises to a few strangers. I recall the raised eyebrows of the chief school building inspector Victor Bwindiki, during our meeting when I had queried procedures for the approval of school-building, and told him I had already built a couple. And my apologies to Tanzanian Immigration, who pointed out that I should have had a Working Permit.

While I was away in Africa, my Canadian lawyer informed me that the first stage of creating a charity organization had been completed; we were now officially registered in B.C. as the *Primary Schools For Africa Society*. The next stage was to apply for official charity status with Canada Revenue Agency, a process that would take at least another six months. I was excited with the progress I'd been briefed about in Tanzania through my emails back and forth to Canada, so I had taken the opportunity, the day before leaving Arusha, to meet again with lawyer Marcellino Mwamnyange, and settle on the process required to get register us as an official NGO in Tanzania.

There is no doubting the extreme need for new schools in Tanzania, and in most developing countries. Many volunteers and NGOs have realized this and have been doing something about it for many years. All one has to do is Google "schools - Africa" to see the incredible work done by dozens of individuals and charities from all over the world. My niece Carolyn e-mailed me to inform me of a schoolteacher, Kathy Lucking, from my hometown of Cornwall, Ontario, who recently funded and organized the construction of a new school in Madagascar. Lynn Connell from Toronto, on a visit to the village of Mto Wa Mbu (interestingly, only a few miles from Gongali), was so moved by the deplorable conditions of an existing orphanage that she went home and raised enough money to transform it into a successful home and school for, at last count, 55 orphans. In the country of Cameroon, on the west coast of Africa, *Schools for Africa*, a charity from England, is working in partnership with another NGO, *SHUMAS*, to prioritize the need for schools, and then build them. They have built dozens of schools there.

My respect and admiration goes out to everyone who is doing something for the disadvantaged, living in extremely isolated and harsh regions, where there is no water or electricity, and where the concept of education is but a remote dream. The logistical challenges are many, but the return that the volunteers receive on their efforts is second to none, and all is made worthwhile. Graduates like Jacob, Claude Goi and Mathew, all from small villages, have returned with the future goal of organizing new schools for their communities.

It is in our hearts to help; to give generously, to volunteer or to fund-raise. It can be easy to convince ourselves of the futility of it all; we think, how can one person make any difference? But for those who believe they can, the rewards are gratifying.

Africa – and all developing countries for that matter – needs more NGOs and volunteers to develop school projects. Hundreds of schools are urgently needed in Tanzania alone, and at present, the government can only rely on private, compassionate individuals, domestic and foreign, to build them. The cost is so small: a $5,000 to $7,000 classroom investment will turn out a graduating class of 45 in seven years. The primary level education that these students will have achieved will allow them to obtain starting employment, for example, as porters, servers and drivers, so they can earn enough income to fund their part-time higher education. At least a few of the 45 will eventually graduate from secondary and university levels with the skills to make a vast difference for their village, community and country.

Education is a powerful tool. Although the path to a better life for countless Tanzanians may seem as insurmountable as the final steep slopes of Mount Kilimanjaro, in the same way that Suranga achieved his ascent by focusing on one step at a time, so can we help Tanzania's children get an education and help achieve their country's lofty goals, one new school at a time.

ACKNOWLEDGEMENTS

Writing this book, a daunting first for me, was akin to being adrift in unknown waters. It was made considerably easier with the help of family, friends and new relationships with professionals who provided the proper charts and compass headings, explained the language of the buoys and markers, and when seas got rough, suggested throwing anchor to restow fallen gear. To the following persons, I am truly thankful and forever indebted. First and foremost, my loving wife Maureen, the brightest beacon in my life, true to her name's meaning, "Star of the Sea", wholeheartedly supported and encouraged me to chase this dream. Danielle Bassett, my stepson Steve's girlfriend who volunteered to do the first round of edits, actually enjoyed the book, especially some of the humorous incidents. Yasuko Thanh, award-winning author, did the second round of edits, allowing me the opportunity to learn from a talented and accomplished professional. Marsha and Bruce Batchelor of Agio Publishing House, with their fresh look and surprising creativity, expertly transformed my crude composition into a respectable document.

Without the passionate contributions of Jacob Slaa Xwatsal and Mathew Gabriel Sulle, who unselfishly volunteered their time in organizing the construction of the schools and helped me transcend the language and cultural barriers, the projects could not have been completed. Most significantly, I am indebted to the Tanzanian people, in particular, the scores of innocently-faced children that I have met in the course of my travels in their magnificent country, for the inspiration they have given me to alter my course in life. They have helped me understand that we are one global family that must share the responsibilities of making this world a more safe, humane and healthy environment so that all families can raise their children with dignity. The Dalai Lama says it quite simply:

"To help guide our global family in the right direction,

good wishes are not sufficient;

we must become actively engaged."

ABOUT THE AUTHOR

ALAN R. ROY

Alan Roy grew up in Cornwall, Ontario. After graduating from Royal Military College, he spent four years in various Canadian and overseas postings. His architectural degrees from the University of New South Wales and RAIC Syllabus preceded 32 years in the architectural profession, the last 15 with his own firm. His previous memorable humanitarian experience was working with ex-president Jimmy Carter in the Lower East Side *Habitat For Humanity* project in New York City. He lives with his wife Maureen, a nurse clinician, in Victoria, B.C., where he has established the office for the new charity, *Primary Schools For Africa Society*.